# Really Interesting Stuff for Kids

*1,500 Fascinating and Educational Facts*

David Fickes

Printed in the United States of America

First Printing: 2019

# Introduction

By nature, I tend to collect trivia without trying. Until relatively recently, I had never sought out trivia; however, after creating a holiday trivia presentation for a community party and then showing it at one of our fitness studio's spinning classes, I found myself creating weekly trivia. The cycling clients enjoyed the diversion of answering questions while they exercised, so I continued.

With this book, I have taken all the accumulated trivia from my other books and selected the content I think is most entertaining and educational for kids. Since I didn't see any reason to state the content differently for a younger audience, the only difference is the trivia selection. To be both entertaining and educational for kids, the facts are heavy on animals, geography, history, and science and nature.

This is book 3 of my *Really Interesting Stuff* series; I hope you enjoy it, and if you do, look for other books in the series.

# Contents

# Facts 1-300

1) Based on oxygen usage, the jellyfish is the most efficient swimmer of any animal. Jellyfish use 48% less oxygen than any other known animal; they never stop moving.

2) Damascus, Syria, is widely regarded as the oldest continuously inhabited city in the world; it has been inhabited for at least 11,000 years.

3) One million dollars in $100 bills weighs about 20.4 pounds.

4) You would get vitamin A poisoning and could die if you ate a polar bear's liver. Polar bears have 50-60 times the normal human levels of vitamin A in their liver, and it is about three times the tolerable level that a human can intake.

5) Moscow, Russia, has the world's busiest McDonald's restaurant.

6) In 1893, New Zealand was the first country to allow women to vote.

7) Relative to its size, the chameleon has the longest tongue of any animal.

8) Cats can't taste sweet. They don't have taste receptors for sweet; this applies to all cats, domestic and wild.

9) Walnuts, almonds, pecans, and cashews aren't technically nuts; they are drupes, which also include peaches, plums, and cherries. Drupes are a type of fruit where an outer fleshy part surrounds a shell or pit with a seed inside. For some drupes, you eat the fleshy part, and for some, you eat the seed inside.

10) For a few seconds, a horse can generate about 15 hp; for sustained output over hours, a horse can generate about 1 hp.

11) With 17 million units sold, the Commodore 64, introduced in 1982 with a 1 MHz processor and 64K of memory, is the biggest selling personal computer model of all time.

12) Gold is the most malleable naturally occurring metal.

13) Mount Chimborazo, Ecuador, is closer to the moon than any other place on the earth. It is 20,548 feet elevation but very close to the equator, so the bulge in the earth makes it 1.5 miles closer to the moon than Mount Everest.

14) The jawbone is the hardest bone in the human body.

15) When a woodpecker's beak hits a tree, it experiences 1,000 times the force of gravity.

16) Oklahoma City and Indianapolis are the only two state capitals that include the name of the state.

17) Wi-Fi doesn't stand for anything. It doesn't mean wireless fidelity or anything else; it is just a branding name picked by a company hired for the purpose.

18) Humans have about 5 million olfactory receptors; dogs have about 220 million.

19) If the moon didn't exist, a day on the earth would be 6-8 hours long.

20) Sheep grazed in New York's Central Park until 1934; for fear they would be eaten, they were moved during the Great Depression.

21) Abraham Lincoln's first choice to lead the Union army was Robert E. Lee.

22) Pure water isn't a good conductor of electricity; the impurities in water make it a good conductor.

23) The Bluetooth wireless technology is named after King Harald "Bluetooth" Gormsson, who ruled Denmark in the 10th century.

24) Deion Sanders is the only person to ever play in the Super Bowl and World Series.

25) The Ruppell's Griffon vulture is the highest-flying bird species ever recorded. They have been spotted at 37,000 feet and have special hemoglobin that makes their oxygen intake more effective.

26) In the Grimm's fairy tale, the *Pied Piper of Hamelin* is described as pied because he wears a two-colored coat; pied is thought to come from magpie birds, which are black and white.

27) While floating in lunar orbit, astronaut Al Worden became the most isolated human ever; he was 2,235 miles from the nearest human while in the *Apollo 15* command module.

28) Catfish have more taste buds than any other animal. They have over 100,000 taste buds, both in their mouth and all over their body; humans have about 10,000.

29) Pikes Peak in Colorado was the inspiration for the song "America the Beautiful."

30) The hippopotamus produces its own sunscreen. It produces a mucus-like secretion that keeps them cool and acts as a powerful sunscreen.

31) Alaska receives the least sunshine of any state.

32) At 700 miles long, Texas and Oklahoma share the longest border of any two states.

33) Saturn is the only planet in our solar system less dense than water.

34) The longest table tennis rally (single point) at an international competition lasted for 2 hours and 12 minutes with an estimated 12,000 hits. It was the opening point of a 1936 world championship match; game time limits were later put in place.

35) The adult human body has about 100,000 miles of blood vessels.

36) Cleopatra was born 2,500 years after the Great Pyramid of Giza was built; she was closer to our current time than she was to the pyramids.

37) California is the only state that is at least partially north of the southernmost part of Canada and at least partially south of the northernmost point of Mexico.

38) Captain Crunch's full name is Captain Horatio Magellan Crunch.

39) Without your pinky finger, you would lose 50% of your hand strength.

40) Extirpation is local extinction; the species is extinct locally but still exists elsewhere.

41) The probability of a human living to 110 years or more is about 1 in 7 million.

42) The bald eagle's name comes from the old English word piebald, meaning white-headed.

43) Due to air resistance, the fastest a human body can fall is about 120 mph; this is known as terminal velocity.

44) The United States has the most domestic cats of any country in the world; China has the second most.

45) At 5.5 million square miles, the Antarctic Polar Desert is the largest desert in the world.

46) Google is the world's most visited website.

47) Kobe Bryant is the only person to win an Olympic gold medal and an Oscar; he won Olympic basketball gold medals in 2008 and 2012 and Best Animated Short Film for *Dear Basketball* (2018).

48) Armadillos are good swimmers, but they also walk underwater to cross bodies of water. They can hold their breath for 6-8 minutes.

49) The most sweat glands on the human body are on the bottom of the feet.

50) Queen Elizabeth II is the longest-reigning British monarch; she surpassed her great-great-grandmother Victoria's reign in 2015.

51) Nevada has the highest percentage of federal land of any state with 81%; Utah is second at 66%.

52) The Incas first domesticated guinea pigs and used them for food, sacrifices, and household pets.

53) Louis Braille developed the Braille system for the blind at the age of 15 and published the first book about it at age 20.

54) Horses can't breathe through their mouths. A soft palate blocks off the pharynx from the mouth, except when swallowing.

55) The tallest mountain in the known universe is 69,459-foot Olympus Mons on Mars.

56) The average person produces 25,000 quarts of saliva in their lifetime.

57) Five surnames have been shared by more than one president: Adams, Harrison, Johnson, Roosevelt, and Bush. Only Andrew and Lyndon Johnson weren't related.

58) Cats are crepuscular animals, which means that they are active primarily during twilight hours, just after dawn and before dusk.

59) In 1942, a German V2 rocket was the first man-made object in space; 62 miles above sea level qualifies as space.

60) Balloons were originally made from animal bladders.

61) Based on land area, Yakutat, Alaska, is the largest city in the United States; at 9,459 square miles, it is larger than the state of New Hampshire.

62) The caribou or reindeer are the only animal species where females have antlers.

63) Five countries have effectively 100% literacy rates: Andorra, Finland, Liechtenstein, Luxembourg, and Norway.

64) Iceland's phone book is alphabetized by first name; everyone is referenced by their first name. They don't have surnames in the traditional sense; the surname is their father's first name suffixed with either son or daughter.

65) If they can't find food, ribbon worms will eat themselves. They can eat a substantial portion of their body and still survive.

66) The dot over the letter "i" is called a tittle.

67) Silver makes up 92.5% of an Olympic gold medal.

68) Pumice is the only rock that floats in water.

69) Butterflies taste with their feet.

70) Adjusted for inflation, *Snow White and the Seven Dwarfs* (1937) is the highest-grossing animated movie of all time in the United States.

71) Under the original terms of the U.S. Constitution, the president didn't choose his vice president; the candidate with the second most electoral votes was vice president.

72) Due to the Mpemba Effect, hot water may freeze faster than cold water; it isn't totally understood why.

73) A lethal dose of chocolate for a human would be about 22 pounds. Theobromine is a powerful stimulant in chocolate and can cause death in high enough doses.

74) A group of rattlesnakes is called a rhumba.

75) Eighty percent of the world's population eats insects as part of their regular diet.

76) Estivation is the summer equivalent to hibernation. During estivation, animals slow their activity for the hot, dry summer months.

77) From 1912 to 1948, the modern Olympics included music, painting, poetry, literature, and architecture.

78) Graca Machel is the only person to be the first lady of two countries. She is the widow of both South Africa President Nelson Mandela and Mozambique President Samora Machel.

79) King Nebuchadnezzar, who built the Hanging Gardens of Babylon, is the best-known historical sufferer of the psychological disorder boanthropy where the sufferer believes they are a cow or ox. In the Book of Daniel, Nebuchadnezzar "was driven from men and did eat grass as oxen."

80) Nauru is the only country in the world without an official capital. It is the third smallest country in the world and has less than 10,000 people.

81) The Greenland shark has the longest known lifespan of all vertebrate (with a backbone) animal species. They can live up to 400 years.

82) The "no animals were harmed" statement on movies only applies when the film is recording.

83) Australia has the world's longest fence; it is the dingo fence; it was completed in 1885 and is 3,488 miles long.

84) At about 65 million years old, Lake Zaysan, in eastern Kazakhstan, is the oldest lake in the world.

85) The opossum has more teeth (50) than any other land mammal.

86) In 1880, Wabash, Indiana, was the world's first electrically lighted city.

87) More English words begin with the letter s than any other letter.

88) The first chocolate treat was hot chocolate during the Aztec civilization.

89) The tardigrade is a water-dwelling, eight-legged, micro animal about 0.02 inches long that can survive extreme conditions that would kill most life forms. They can survive temperatures from -458 to 300 degrees Fahrenheit, pressures from the vacuum of space to more than 1,000 atmospheres, and radiation 1,000 times higher than other animals. They can also live for 30 years without food or water. They were discovered in 1773 and are found everywhere from mountain tops to deep sea and tropical areas to the Antarctic.

90) In September 1989, Deion Sanders hit an MLB home run and scored an NFL touchdown in the same week. He is the only person ever to do it.

91) Silver is the best conductor of electricity of any metal; it is slightly more conductive than copper but much more expensive.

92) *The Simpsons* is the longest-running U.S. scripted primetime show ever; it started in 1989.

93) At age 70, Benjamin Franklin was the oldest person to sign the Declaration of Independence; the average signer was 44 years old.

94) On average, sharks kill 12 people per year worldwide.

95) Leonardo da Vinci could write with both his left and right hand simultaneously.

96) Badminton is the fastest racquet sport; the shuttlecock can travel over 200 mph.

97) The hippopotamus is responsible for the most human deaths of any of the large African animals.

98) Alaska was purchased from Russia in 1867 for two cents per acre.

99) Canada is the only country in the world where more than 50% of its adults have college degrees.

100) There are 108 stitches on a regulation baseball.

101) The ancient Greeks used olive oil instead of soap to clean themselves; they rubbed it into their skin and then scraped it off along with dirt and dead skin.

102) The greatest distance any human has ever been from the earth is 248,655 miles aboard *Apollo 13*.

103) About 88% of the world's population lives in the Northern Hemisphere. About half of the world's population lives north of 27 degrees north latitude.

104) Four presidential candidates have won the popular vote but lost the election: Andrew Jackson against John Quincy Adams, Samuel Tilden against Rutherford B. Hayes, Al Gore against George W. Bush, and Hilary Clinton against Donald Trump.

105) A starfish is the only creature that can turn its stomach inside out.

106) In total darkness, most people naturally adjust to a 48-hour cycle, instead of 24 hours. They have 36 hours of activity followed by 12 hours of sleep; the reasons are unclear.

107) A kangaroo can hop at 40 mph.

108) Venus and Uranus are the only two planets in our solar system that rotate clockwise.

109) After the cheetah, the pronghorn antelope is the second fastest land animal. Pronghorns can achieve speeds of 55 mph.

110) Sunglasses were invented in China to hide the eyes of judges.

111) The Atlantic Ocean is the saltiest ocean.

112) By area, Manitoulin Island, in Lake Huron, Ontario, Canada, is the largest freshwater island in the world; it is over 1,000 square miles.

113) The ostrich is the fastest two-legged animal; it can reach speeds over 40 mph.

114) A priest was the first person to propose the big bang origin of the universe; Georges Lemaitre's work preceded Edwin Hubble.

115) It would take 1.2 million mosquitoes, each sucking once, to drain the average human of all their blood.

116) The earth is the densest planet in our solar system.

117) Of the earth's total water, 96.5% is in the oceans.

118) The four states of matter observable in everyday life are solid, liquid, gas, and plasma.

119) The sun orbits around the center of the Milky Way Galaxy at a speed of 536,865 mph.

120) With 800 languages spoken, New York City is the most linguistically diverse (highest number of languages spoken) city in the world.

121) Captain James Cook was the first man to set foot on all the continents other than Antarctica.

122) Kiribati is the only country that falls in all four hemispheres; it is an island nation in the central Pacific.

123) The original name for Los Angeles was El Pueblo de Nuestra Señora la Reina de los Ángeles del Río Porciúncula.

124) The Indonesian word for water is air.

125) At 22,595 feet, Ojos Del Salado, on the Chile & Argentina border, is the highest active volcano in the world.

126) The highest percentage of Americans are sleeping at 3:00 am, about 95.1%.

127) A human can live unprotected in space for about 30 seconds, provided they don't hold their breath. You would be unconscious in about 15 seconds; if you hold your breath, your lungs explode.

128) Peppermint was the first Lifesaver flavor.

129) Humans need 16 to 20 images per second to perceive something as a moving picture, rather than a flickering image; dogs need 70 images per second. Older televisions could only produce 50 images per second, so dogs would only see flickering images; modern televisions are fast enough to appear as moving pictures to dogs.

130) William Howard Taft was the heaviest U.S. president; he weighed about 340 pounds when he left office.

131) If you hear thunder about 15 seconds after seeing lightning, the lightning is about 3 miles away. Sound travels about one mile in five seconds.

132) The average person spends three months of their life sitting on the toilet.

133) Forty is the only number spelled out in English that has its letters in alphabetical order.

134) In 1983, Guion Bluford was the first African American in space.

135) The Statue of Liberty's shoe size would be 879.

136) In 1960, Sri Lanka was the first nation to have a female prime minister.

137) Paraguay is the only country with a two-sided (different designs on each side) flag.

138) The blanket octopus has the largest size difference between males and females of any non-microscopic animal. Females are 10,000 to 40,000 times larger than males; females can be 6.5 feet in length; males are 1 inch.

139) The Maldives is the lowest elevation country in the world; it is composed of 1,200 mostly uninhabited islands in the Indian Ocean with a maximum elevation of six feet.

140) Educated people have believed the earth was round for about 2,500 years. Pythagoras postulated the earth was round in the 6th century BC; Aristotle agreed it was round in the 4th century BC.

141) Bamboo is the fastest growing plant; certain species can grow three feet in a day

142) Of all the people in the world who have ever lived to 65 years old, about two-thirds are alive today.

143) The word set has the most definitions of any English word; set has 464 definitions in the Oxford English Dictionary; run is second with 396 definitions.

144) The U.S. icon Uncle Sam was based on Samuel Wilson, who was a meatpacker during the War of 1812. He supplied barrels of beef to the army stamped with "U.S.," indicating the United States, but soldiers started referring to it as Uncle Sam's.

145) The thinnest skin on the human body is the eyelid. It is 0.05 mm thick; the palms and soles of feet are the thickest at 1.5 mm.

146) Dogs have 13 blood types; humans only have four.

147) Dr. Seuss wrote *Green Eggs and Ham* after his editor dared him to write a book using fewer than 50 different words.

148) The Harlem Globetrotters are the only sports team to play on all seven continents.

149) Subway has the most locations worldwide of any fast food franchise.

150) *Toy Story* (1995) was the word's first computer-animated feature film.

151) Presidents Thomas Jefferson and John Adams both died on July 4, 1826.

152) Sacagawea has more statues in her honor than anyone else in the United States.

153) The spire on the Empire State building was meant to be used as an airship dock.

154) If not limited to the major parties, over 200 women have run for U.S. president.

155) Annapolis, Maryland, and Albany, New York, are the only two state capitals named for royalty. Annapolis is named for Princess Anne of Denmark and Norway, who became Queen of England; Albany is named for the Duke of York and Albany, who became King James II of England.

156) The United Kingdom and Great Britain are not the same; Great Britain includes England, Scotland, and Wales; the United Kingdom also includes Northern Ireland.

157) Thirteen states are entirely north of the southernmost point of Canada: Alaska, Washington, Oregon, Idaho, Montana, North Dakota, South Dakota, Minnesota, Wisconsin, Michigan, Vermont, New Hampshire, and Maine.

158) Antarctica has the largest volcanic region; there is an area of over 100 volcanoes under the ice sheet in western Antarctica.

159) Only one species of insect is native to Antarctica, the Antarctic midge.

160) Over 80 women worldwide have been elected or appointed head of their country.

161) Until the 1770s, de-crusted, moistened, and balled-up bread was used to erase lead pencil marks.

162) Mosquitoes like blood type O the most. They prefer it twice as much as type A; type B is their second choice.

163) McDonald's is by far the largest toy distributor in the world; about 20% of its meals are Happy Meals with a toy.

164) The Eiffel Tower is the most-visited paid monument in the world.

165) H.G. Wells coined the term "atomic bomb" approximately 30 years before its invention.

166) Manon Rheaume was the first woman to appear in an NHL game. In September 1992, she goaltended for the Tampa Bay Lightning in a pre-season game against the St. Louis Blues.

167) In 1863, a military draft was started to provide troops for the Union army; the draft was set up to allow two ways that you could avoid going. You could pay $300 or find someone else to go in your place; what happened is that people paid $300 to have someone else go in their place. Some people made a career out of taking the money to be a substitute, deserting, and repeating the process.

168) Your glabella is the skin between the eyebrows, just above the nose.

169) Winnie the Pooh's real name is Edward Bear.

170) In bowling, three strikes in a row are called a turkey because late 18th and early 19th-century bowling tournaments gave out food items as tournament prizes. At some point, getting three strikes in a row became associated with winning a turkey, and the name spread and stuck. Due to the much cruder equipment and lanes of long ago, getting three strikes in a row was a very difficult feat.

171) The Egyptian pyramids were built by paid laborers, not slaves.

172) As a republic and a state, Texas has had 12 different capital cities including Galveston, Houston, and Austin.

173) Cats are such picky eaters because they seem to be naturally driven to eat foods with about equal energy from protein and fat. They will seek out these ratios, even overriding taste preferences; science has no idea how they know what food provides the correct ratio.

174) Armadillos always give birth to four identical offspring. As part of their normal reproduction, a single embryo splits into four.

175) Astoria, Oregon is the oldest city west of the Rocky Mountains; it was founded in 1811.

176) In ancient Egypt, the penalty for killing a cat, even accidentally, was death.

177) Greenland is part of the Kingdom of Denmark; it is so large that if you include it as part of Denmark's area, Denmark is the 12th largest country in the world.

178) South Africa is the first nation that created nuclear weapons and then voluntarily got rid of them.

179) The goose was the first bird domesticated by man, more than 4,000 years ago in Egypt.

180) The border between the United States and Mexico is the most frequently crossed international border in the world.

181) Annapolis, Maryland, is the only state capital that was once the national capital.

182) Due to behavioral differences, men are five times more likely than women to be hit by lightning.

183) Scorpions can live up to six days without air; they can also go up to a year without eating.

184) Only three people have won individual gold medals in the same event in four consecutive Olympics: Michael Phelps (swimming 200-meter individual medley), Carl Lewis (long jump), and Al Oerter (discus).

185) The first organ transplants occurred in 800 BC when Indian doctors performed skin grafts.

186) Barbara Bush and Abigail Adams's husbands and sons both served as U.S. president.

187) To allow visitors to travel safely to Olympia, a truce, or ekecheiria, was put in place before and during each of the ancient Olympic games. During this time, wars were suspended; legal disputes were put on hold, and no death penalties were carried out.

188) Your taste buds are replaced every 10-14 days.

189) The Statue of Liberty originally also served as a lighthouse.

190) The last man on the moon was in 1972.

191) The black mamba is the fastest moving land snake; it can move at speeds up to 12 mph.

192) In an average lifetime, human skin completely replaces itself 900 times.

193) When attacked, the horned toad squirts blood from its eyes.

194) In WWII, Italy declared war on both Germany and the Allies; one month after surrendering to the allies, Italy declared war on Germany, its former ally.

195) A dog's DNA is 99.9% the same as a gray wolf.

196) You can tell the age of a whale by counting the rings in its earwax.

197) American Eddie Eagan is the only person to win gold medals in both the winter and summer Olympics. He won for boxing in 1920 and bobsled in 1932.

198) Bears don't urinate while they hibernate. Their body converts the urine into protein, and they use it as food.

199) Red is the most common color on national flags.

200) The peregrine falcon was the first animal placed on the endangered species list.

201) Linus Pauling is the only person to win two unshared Nobel Prizes.

202) The eruption of Mount Tambora volcano, in Indonesia in 1815, is the most powerful explosion ever witnessed on the earth. It was equivalent to 800 megatons of TNT, 14 times larger than the largest man-made explosion.

203) Originally, people bowed to the U.S. president; Thomas Jefferson was the first president to shake hands, rather than bowing.

204) A galactic or cosmic year is the amount of time it takes the sun to orbit once around the center of the Milky Way Galaxy, about 230 million years.

205) About 5,500 WWII bombs are still discovered in Germany each year.

206) Alaska has the largest number of active volcanoes of any state; 130 out of the 169 active volcanoes in the United States are in Alaska.

207) Canada has a longer coastline than the rest of the world combined. At 125,567 miles, Canada's coastline is 3.5 times longer than any other country.

208) The left leg of a chicken is more tender than the right. Chickens scratch with their right leg, building up more muscle in that leg and making it tougher than the left.

209) The first African American was elected to serve in the U.S. Congress in 1870; he was a senator from Mississippi.

210) The average person walks about 75,000 miles in their life.

211) Before 1938, toothbrushes were made using boar hairs.

212) Morocco has the world's oldest continuously operating university; it has existed since 859 AD.

213) There is enough gold in the earth's core to coat the entire surface of the earth to a depth of 1.5 feet.

214) Giraffes have seven neck vertebrae, the same as humans.

215) The megalodon shark is thought to be the largest shark that ever lived. It became extinct about 2.6 million years ago and was up to 59 feet long and weighed 65 tons.

216) Sharks don't get cavities because the outside of their teeth is made of fluoride.

217) The blue whale is the largest animal ever known to have lived on the earth. They can be up to 100 feet long and weigh 200 tons.

218) Excluding man, dolphins have the longest tested memory. Bottlenose dolphins have unique whistles; studies have shown that they remember the whistle of other dolphins they have lived with, even after 20 years of separation.

219) Monaco is the capital of Monaco; it is both a city and a country.

220) By area, Lake Michigan is the largest lake entirely within the United States.

221) The human ears and nose never stop growing.

222) The can opener was invented 45 years after tin cans were invented.

223) Iguanas have three eyes. They have a third parietal eye on top of their head that can just distinguish light and dark.

224) The frisbee was originally called the Pluto Platter.

225) Florida is the flattest state; there are only 345 feet between its highest and lowest elevations.

226) Twelve American prisoners of war were killed in the Hiroshima atomic bomb blast.

227) Saffron is made from crocus flowers; only the stigma part of the flower is used. It takes 70,000 to 250,000 flowers to make one pound of saffron, which is why it is so expensive.

228) A newborn human baby has about one cup of blood in their body.

229) Aluminum is the major constituent of rubies.

230) Chocolate is the only edible substance that melts just below human body temperature. Chocolate melts at 93 degrees, which is why it melts in your mouth.

231) Adjusted for inflation, *Snow White and the Seven Dwarfs* (1937) is the earliest movie made that has grossed $1 billion in the United States.

232) Notre Dame Cathedral was almost demolished in the 19th century but was saved by Victor Hugo's *The Hunchback of Notre Dame*; Hugo wrote the novel partially to save the cathedral from demolition.

233) The clavicle (collar bone) is the most frequently broken bone in the human body.

234) Research has shown that most mammals on average live for about 1.5 billion heartbeats. Larger animals have slower heartbeats, so they live longer; humans used to fit the pattern but with health and medical improvements, we last longer than our size predicts. At 60 beats per minute, 1.5 billion heartbeats would be 47.5 years.

235) The "DC" in DC Comics stands for Detective Comics.

236) The king cobra is the only snake that builds a nest. They can lay up to 40 eggs at once; the nest is built from vegetation and helps keep the eggs safe.

237) The earth orbits around the sun at 66,600 mph.

238) St. Augustine, Florida, is the oldest city in the United States; it was founded in 1565.

239) The heat of a bolt of lightning is about five times hotter than the surface of the sun.

240) Malaria is believed to have killed more people than any other disease throughout history; it still kills about 1 million people annually.

241) At 5'4", James Madison was the shortest president.

242) The whale shark has the world's largest egg, up to 12 inches long; the ostrich has the largest laid egg.

243) In 5 BC, Rome was the first city to reach a population of 1 million people.

244) Great Smoky Mountains is the most visited U.S. National Park.

245) During WWII, Queen Elizabeth II served as a mechanic and driver.

246) Belgium invented French fried potatoes in the late 17th century.

247) The Barbie doll's full name is Barbara Millicent Roberts.

248) The world's most popular first name is Mohammed and its variations.

249) Australia has the world's largest feral camel herd, as many as 1 million camels at one point. They were imported in the 19th century, and many were later set free as the automobile took over; they now roam freely with no natural predators.

250) Amen means "So be it" in Hebrew.

251) A googolplexian is the largest named number. A googol is one followed by 100 zeroes; a googolplex is one followed by a googol of zeroes; a googolplexian is one followed by a googolplex of zeroes.

252) The population density of ancient Rome was about eight times greater than in modern New York City.

253) The kori bustard is the heaviest bird capable of flight. They are from Africa and can weigh over 40 pounds.

254) A group of bears is called a sloth.

255) The tortoise is the longest living land animal of any kind; the oldest known lived to 250.

256) As soon as sand tiger shark embryos develop teeth while still in the womb, the largest of the embryos in each of the two uteruses attacks and eats its siblings, leaving just two pups to be born.

257) Ambisinistrous means no good with either hand; it is the opposite of ambidextrous.

258) Arabic numerals were first used in India.

259) Only one person in modern recorded history has been struck dead by a meteorite. In 2016 in India, a 40-year-old man was relaxing outside on the grounds of a small engineering college when there was the sound of an explosion; he was found next to a two-foot crater and later succumbed to injuries sustained.

260) William Howard Taft is the only man that was both Chief Justice of the U.S. Supreme Court and U.S. president.

261) The hyoid bone in the throat is the only bone in the human body that isn't attached to any other bone.

262) Based on land area, Jacksonville, Florida, is the largest city in the 48 contiguous states at 758 square miles.

263) A cat's jaw can't move sideways, so they can't chew large chunks.

264) There are 42 eyes in a deck of 52 cards. The jack of hearts, jack of spades, and the king of diamonds are in profile, with only one eye showing.

265) Virginia is the most common U.S. president's birth state, with eight presidents.

266) Four people have won two Nobel prizes: Marie Curie, Linus Pauling, John Bardeen, and Frederick Sanger.

267) Aristarchus of Samos first proposed that the sun was the center around which the planets orbit in the 3rd century BC; Copernicus developed a fully predictive model in the 16th century but wasn't the first to propose the concept.

268) The Monday before and the Wednesday after the MLB All-Star game are the only two days during the year where there are no MLB, NFL, NHL, or NBA games played. The MLB All-Star game is always played on a Tuesday, and there are no MLB games the day before or after, and MLB is the only professional sport played in July.

269) English has more words than any other language.

270) Mary Edwards Walker is the only woman ever awarded the U.S. Medal of Honor; she received it for her service in the Civil War. She was a surgeon at a temporary Washington, D.C. hospital and was captured and arrested as a spy after crossing enemy lines to treat wounded civilians.

271) At their closest point, Europe and Africa are separated by nine miles between Spain and Morocco.

272) Oscar the Grouch, from television's *Sesame Street*, was originally orange.

273) In 1678, Elena Cornaro Piscopia was the first woman in the world to receive a PhD degree.

274) If you search for the word askew in Google, the content comes back tilted to the right.

275) Up until 800 years ago, New Zealand was undiscovered and devoid of humans.

276) Cleopatra was the last Pharaoh of Egypt.

277) From the Middle Ages until 1809, Finland was part of Sweden.

278) The average person spends about six years of their life dreaming.

279) The most common time to wake up in the middle of the night is 3:44 am.

280) The United States, Liberia, and Myanmar are the only three countries that don't use the metric system.

281) The average lightning bolt is about five miles long and one inch wide.

282) Camels have three eyelids to protect them from the sand.

283) Hotfoot Teddy was the original name of Smokey the Bear.

284) Tooth enamel is the hardest substance in the human body.

285) On average, the moon is 238,900 miles from the earth.

286) The first cell phone call was made in 1973.

287) The average chocolate bar has eight insect parts.

288) Joseph A. Walker was the first person to fly into space twice; he did it in 1963 aboard an X-15 winged aircraft. Space is defined as 100 km or 62 miles above the earth.

289) During the American Civil War, women were prohibited from enlisting in both the Union and Confederate armies, but more than 600 women, dressed as men, joined the war anyway.

290) Kenyon College won the NCAA Division III men's swimming and diving championship for 31 consecutive years from 1980-2010. It is the most consecutive national championships for any men's or women's team in any NCAA division.

291) Less than a year before Abraham Lincoln was assassinated, his oldest son, Robert, was saved from being hit by a train by Edwin Booth, the brother of John Wilkes Booth.

292) Hydrogen is the most abundant element in the universe; it accounts for about 75% of the universe's mass.

293) Australia is the only country with all 10 of the deadliest snakes in the world.

294) The Snickers candy bar is named after the creator's horse.

295) Almost half the gold ever mined has come from Witwatersrand, South Africa.

296) Of all the text information stored on the world's computers, 80% is in English.

297) Rhythms is the longest common English word without any vowels.

298) Human life expectancy has increased more in the last 50 years than it has in the prior 200,000 years.

299) The word scientist was first used in 1833.

300) A cricket's ears are located on its front legs.

# Facts 301-600

301) A giraffe cleans its ears with its tongue.

302) Queen Elizabeth II is the largest landowner in the world; she technically owns 6.6 billion acres, about one-sixth of the world's land including Canada and Australia.

303) Each year, 15,000 to 18,000 new animal species are discovered; about half are insects.

304) Washington, D.C., has a smaller percentage of the country's population than any other national capital in the world; it has just 0.21% of the U.S. population.

305) You could fit 1.3 million Earths inside the sun, an average-size star.

306) Russia is the third closest country to the United States.

307) Horseshoe crab blood is worth $14,000 per quart because its unique chemical properties make it very valuable for bacterial testing. It can coagulate around as little as one part in a trillion of bacterial contamination, and the reaction only takes 45 minutes, instead of two days with mammalian blood.

308) The Antarctic ice sheet has 90% of the earth's freshwater; it is equivalent to about 230 feet of water in the world's oceans.

309) The human eye can differentiate more shades of green than any other color; that is why night vision goggles are green.

310) At age 42, Theodore Roosevelt is the youngest-ever U.S. president; John F. Kennedy is the youngest elected president at age 43.

311) Leeches have 32 brains; each controls a different segment of their body.

312) The whip was the first man-made object to break the sound barrier. The crack a whip makes is due to a small sonic boom.

313) The most commonly spoken word in the world is OK.

314) The U.S. film industry relocated from New York to Los Angeles in large part because of Thomas Edison; he held many of the patents on the production and showing of movies and controlled the industry. Filmmakers escaped to Los Angeles to get away from his control.

315) William Henry Harrison had the shortest term as U.S. president, just 31 days; he caught a cold on inauguration day that turned into a fatal case of pneumonia. His grandson Benjamin would later also be president.

316) Park is the most popular street name in the United States.

317) The sperm whale produces the loudest sound of any animal. It can reach 230 decibels; a rock concert is 150 decibels.

318) Detartrated is the longest palindrome word in English; palindromes are the same forward and backward.

319) A polar bear can swim 60 miles without stopping.

320) Pork is the most widely-eaten meat in the world; poultry is second; beef is third.

321) In 1891, Whitcomb Judson invented the zipper for fastening shoes.

322) The tallest tsunami wave ever recorded was in Lituya Bay, Alaska, in 1958; it was 1,720 feet tall. An 8.0 earthquake dropped 40 to 50 million cubic yards of rock and ice 3,000 feet down into the bay, creating the wave.

323) China has the most countries or territories bordering it; there are 14 countries and 2 territories.

324) By area, Michigan is 41.5% water, the highest percentage of any state.

325) In its natural form, aspirin comes from the bark of the white willow tree.

326) Phoenix, Arizona, has the largest population of any state capital.

327) Mexican War hero Zachary Taylor was the first man with no political experience to be elected U.S. president.

328) The term "sweat like a pig" comes from the iron smelting process and has nothing to do with pigs sweating. During the process, molten iron was poured into molds with ingots branching off a central channel that reminded people of piglets suckling on a sow, so the iron became known as pig iron. When the pig iron was cool enough to transport, it would sweat from condensation from the air, giving the term "sweat like a pig."

329) Bananas are the most widely eaten fruit in the United States; apples are second.

330) Four state capitals are named after presidents: Lincoln, Jefferson City, Jackson, and Madison.

331) Based on AKC registrations, the three most popular purebred dogs in the United States are the Labrador Retriever, German Shepherd, and Golden Retriever.

332) On average, most people have fewer friends than their friends have; this is known as the friendship paradox. You are more likely to be friends with someone who has more friends than someone who has fewer friends.

333) The Great Pyramid of Giza has eight sides; each of the four sides is split from base to tip by slight concave indentations, creating eight sides. The indentations were first noticed by a pilot flying over in 1940.

334) Scientists believe that herrings use farts to communicate. Herrings have excellent hearing, and their farts produce a high-pitched sound. The farts are from gulping air at the surface and storing it in their swim bladder.

335) Grover Cleveland is the only president to serve two non-consecutive terms; he was the 22nd and 24th president.

336) Theodore Roosevelt was the first president to leave the United States while in office; he went to Panama to inspect the construction of the canal.

337) Mexico has the highest annual average hours worked in the world.

338) The main reason for the character layout of the qwerty keyboard we use today is to prevent typewriter jams by placing often used keys further apart.

339) Cats have more than 100 vocal sounds; dogs only have about 10.

340) Ulaanbaatar, Mongolia, is the coldest national capital city in the world; winter temperatures of -40 degrees Fahrenheit are not unusual.

341) A human can live up to 11 days without sleeping.

342) The only U.S. soil that Japan occupied during WWII were two remote Aleutian Islands; the United States battled Japan to retake the islands between June 1942 and August 1943.

343) U.S. President John Tyler had 15 children by two different wives.

344) Lebanon is the only Middle Eastern country without a desert.

345) Uzbekistan and Liechtenstein are the only two countries completely surrounded by landlocked countries.

346) Time is the most commonly used noun in the English language.

347) Of cities of 1 million or more population, Auckland, New Zealand, is furthest away from another city of 1 million population or more; it is 1,347 miles away from Sydney, Australia.

348) George Washington and James Monroe are the only two men that have run effectively unopposed for U.S. president.

349) Ecuador is the only point on the equator with snow on the ground.

350) Maine is the closest state to Africa; Quoddy Head, Maine, is 3,154 miles from Morocco. It is almost 1,000 miles closer than Florida.

351) The project that would become the Statue of Liberty was originally conceived of as a peasant Muslim woman in traditional dress. The statue was originally intended for Egypt before they turned the project down, and it was redesigned for the United States.

352) If you weigh 150 pounds on the earth, you will weigh 4,200 pounds on the sun.

353) Adult domestic cats only meow to communicate with humans. They don't meow to each other; it is thought to be a post-domestication extension of kittens mewing.

354) In 1916, Germany was the first country to implement daylight saving time to save energy during WWI.

355) A human fart travels about 7 mph.

356) Calvin Coolidge is the only president born on the 4th of July.

357) A group of cats is called a clowder.

358) Ninety percent of all meteorites ever found come from Antarctica.

359) The average cumulus cloud weighs 1.1 million pounds.

360) President Andrew Jackson was shot at twice at point-blank range but survived because both guns misfired; it was the first assassination attempt against a U.S. president.

361) Piggy banks got their name because they were originally made from pygg clay. The clay was used to make bowls and jars and other containers that people started to store change in; the containers were not made into pig shapes until much later.

362) Hong Kong has more skyscrapers than any other city in the world; New York City is second; Dubai is third. There is no exact definition of a skyscraper, but they are generally considered to be 150 meters or taller.

363) On *Sesame Street*, the Cookie Monster's real name is Sid.

364) President James Buchanan was morally opposed to slavery but believed it was protected by the constitution, so he bought slaves with his own money and freed them.

365) The lens of the eye continues to grow throughout a person's life.

366) North Dakota is the geographic center of North America.

367) The shortest complete English sentence is "Go."

368) Q is the least used letter in the English alphabet.

369) Of all the animal species scientists have studied, domestic cats are the only one that shows no outward signs of conciliatory behavior.

370) The highest percentage of Americans are awake at 6:00 pm, about 97.5%.

371) Andrew Johnson is the only president that made their own clothes; he had been a tailor's apprentice and opened a tailor shop. He made his own clothes for most of his life.

372) The U.S. $10,000 bill was last printed in 1945 and is the largest denomination ever in public circulation; Salmon P. Chase, Secretary of the Treasury, had his portrait on it.

373) The V-shaped formation of a flock of geese is called a skein.

374) A rhinoceros' horn is made of hair.

375) There were eight U.S. national capital cities before Washington, D.C.: Philadelphia, Pennsylvania; Baltimore, Maryland; Lancaster Pennsylvania; York, Pennsylvania; Princeton, New Jersey; Annapolis, Maryland; Trenton, New Jersey; and New York City, New York.

376) Papua New Guinea has the largest number of languages spoken of any country; it has about 850 languages, one for every 8,000 citizens.

377) Missouri and Tennessee share the most borders with other states; each one borders eight other states.

378) The sperm whale dives deeper and stays underwater longer than any other whale. They can dive for more than an hour and more than 4,000 feet deep.

379) Feeding on krill, blue whales can consume 500,000 calories in a single mouthful.

380) France and its territories cover more time zones than any other country. France has 12 times zones; the United States and Russia and their territories each cover 11 time zones.

381) After man, the longest living land mammal is the elephant; the oldest known lived to 86.

382) With speeds up to 68 mph, the sailfish is the fastest fish.

383) Almost one-third of the world's languages are only spoken in Africa.

384) The word goodbye is a contraction of "God be with ye."

385) The greatest distance on the earth between the nearest points of land is 994 miles from Bouvet Island in the South Atlantic to Antarctica.

386) Relative to its body size, the cockroach is possibly the largest methane producer; they emit up to 43 times their weight in methane annually.

387) The human eye can distinguish about 10 million colors.

388) All the gold ever mined would fit in four Olympic swimming pools.

389) San Marino has the oldest surviving constitution in the world; it dates to 1600. The U.S. constitution is the second oldest.

390) In 1892, Gallaudet University, a school for the deaf, originated the football huddle. They huddled to avoid the other team seeing their sign language.

391) John Tyler was the first vice president to become president upon the death of a president; he succeeded William Henry Harrison, who died of pneumonia 31 days into his presidency.

392) Melania Trump, Michelle Obama, and Eleanor Roosevelt are tied as the tallest U.S. first ladies at 5'11".

393) Osmium is the densest naturally occurring element; it is about 25 times denser than water.

394) A rat can fall 50 feet uninjured.

395) Australia has the largest population of poisonous snakes of any country.

396) George Washington and Benjamin Franklin appeared on the first U.S. postage stamps issued in 1847.

397) Russia has 11 time zones; it spans over 5,700 miles east to west.

398) In Victorian London, people were paid to collect dog poop for use in tanning leather.

399) The largest national park in the world is in Greenland. The Northeast Greenland National Park is 375,000 square miles; it is about 100 times bigger than Yellowstone National Park and only has about 500 visitors per year.

400) A day on Mars is 40 minutes longer than a day on Earth.

401) Japan and Russia still haven't officially signed a peace treaty between them ending WWII; they have a dispute over the Kuril Islands.

402) A blue moon is defined as the second full moon in a calendar month. It happens about every three years, giving the expression "once in a blue moon" for something that doesn't occur very often.

403) During WWI, the British tried to train seagulls to poop on the periscopes of enemy submarines.

404) In terms of production volume, tomatoes are the most popular fruit in the world.

405) Before the 20th century, lobster was considered a mark of poverty and was used for fertilizer and fed to slaves. Its reputation changed when modern transportation allowed shipping live lobsters to urban centers.

406) At President Andrew Jackson's funeral in 1845, his pet parrot was removed for swearing.

407) In terms of how long it takes to process the input, the fastest human sense is hearing; it takes as little as 0.05 seconds to process.

408) At 5,525 miles, the United States and Canada share the longest land border in the world.

409) Sapphires are the second hardest gem after diamonds.

410) As originally written, Aladdin is Chinese.

411) The seahorse and pipefish are the only two species of fish where the male gives birth.

412) A blue whale's pulse is 8-10 beats per minute.

413) Sphenopalatine ganglioneuralgia is the medical term for a brain freeze, also known as ice cream headache.

414) Indonesia has the most earthquakes of any country; Japan has the second most.

415) Depending on conditions, the lifespan of a housefly is 15-30 days.

416) The Amazon is the widest river in the world; it is almost 25 miles wide during the wet season.

417) During the 18th century, you could pay for your admission to the London zoo by bringing a cat or dog to feed the lions.

418) Q is the only letter that doesn't appear in any state name.

419) The earliest pillows date back 9,000 years to Mesopotamia; they were made from stone, with a curved top, and were designed to keep the head off the ground and prevent insects from crawling into the mouth, nose, and ears.

420) The pineal gland in the center of the brain is the smallest organ in the human body; it is about the size of a grain of rice.

421) At 243 Earth days, Venus has the longest day of any planet in our solar system.

422) At 2,700 miles, Alaska is the widest state from east to west.

423) On April 10, 1996, Tropical Cyclone Olivia produced a 253 mph wind on Barrow Island, Australia, the world's highest surface wind speed ever recorded.

424) Switzerland and Vatican City are the only two countries with square flags.

425) Bees have five eyes; they have two large, compound eyes on the sides of their head and three simple eyes on the top of their head.

426) Eleven U.S. states are larger than the United Kingdom.

427) Killer whales aren't actually whales; they are dolphins. Their similarities with dolphins include teeth, streamlined bodies, rounded head, beak, echolocation, living in pods, and group hunting.

428) The year 1 BC was followed by 1 AD.

429) Warren G. Harding had the largest feet, size 14, of any U.S. president.

430) Wyoming has only two escalators in the entire state.

431) The Sargasso Sea is the only sea without a coastline (no land border). It is in the North Atlantic off the coast of the United States and is defined by currents.

432) Maine is the only state that borders just one other state.

433) Of all countries that aren't landlocked, Monaco has the shortest coastline, 2.4 miles.

434) The earliest surviving written music dates to 1400 BC, it was a hymn found in Syria.

435) A month beginning on a Sunday always has a Friday the 13th.

436) A cockroach can live a week without its head. They are not dependent on their head or mouth to breathe, but they will eventually die without it because they can't drink and die of thirst.

437) The world's smallest natural trees are dwarf willows that grow in Greenland and are only about two inches high.

438) Twelve people have walked on the moon, but only three have been to the deepest part of the ocean. Director James Cameron is one of the three.

439) China has about half of all the pigs in the world.

440) The point in the ocean furthest from the nearest land is 1,670 miles from land; it is called Point Nemo and is in the South Pacific.

441) An elephant has 40,000 muscles in its trunk; there are about 640 muscles in the entire human body.

442) Hummingbirds have the biggest brain relative to their body size of any bird. Their brain is over 4% of their body weight.

443) St. Lucia is the only country in the world named after a woman; it is in the Caribbean and is named after St. Lucy of Syracuse, who lived in the 3rd century.

444) Koalas are the sleepiest animal in the world; they sleep 22 hours per day.

445) Shark skin was once used commercially as sandpaper.

446) Leonardo da Vinci was the first person to explain why the sky is blue.

447) Russian astronauts take guns into space to protect themselves from bears if they land off course.

448) Woodrow Wilson is the only president with a PhD; he had a doctorate in history and political science.

449) The McMurdo Dry Valleys of Antarctica are the driest place on the earth; they are a row of snow-free valleys that haven't seen water in millions of years.

450) Since it is exposed to the sun a lot of the time while they eat, a giraffe's tongue is black or purple to prevent sunburn.

451) Yellowstone National Park has most of the world's geysers.

452) Taumatawhakatangihangakoauauotamateaturipukakapikimaunga -horonukupokaiwhenuakitanatahu is the longest place name in the world; it is a hill in New Zealand.

453) Almost 100% of kangaroos are left-handed.

454) At 59.9 degrees north latitude, St. Petersburg, Russia, is the northernmost city in the world with a population of over 1 million.

455) Including hunting dives, the peregrine falcon is the fastest bird in the world, with speeds up to 242 mph.

456) There were 20 years between the first female in space and the first American female in space. Soviet Valentina Tereshkova was the first in 1963; Sally Ride was the first American in 1983.

457) With over 300,000 people, Murmansk, Russia, is the most populous city north of the Arctic Circle.

458) The first automobile speeding ticket was issued in 1896 in England. The car was going 8 mph; the speed limit for cars was 2 mph. You could go over 2 mph if you had someone walk in front of the car waving a red flag to alert people.

459) Of the 700 islands in the Bahamas, only 30 are inhabited.

460) The Fahrenheit and Celsius temperature scales are the same at 40 degrees below zero.

461) Humans and dogs are the only two animal species known to seek visual clues from another animal's eyes, and dogs only do it with humans.

462) Venus is often called the Earth's twin because it is nearly the same size and mass and has a similar composition.

463) A newborn Bactrian camel doesn't have any humps. Baby camels don't get their humps until they start eating solid food.

464) Pierre, South Dakota, is the only state capital that doesn't share any letters with its state.

465) The Caspian Sea is the largest enclosed inland body of water in the world; it is considered a lake by some, but it has saltwater. It has 3.5 times more water than all the Great Lakes combined.

466) Lesotho is the only country that lies completely above 1,000 meters elevation; it is 11,720 square miles and is completely surrounded by South Africa.

467) The national capital city of La Paz, Bolivia, is one of the most fire-safe cities in the world. At an elevation of 11,800 feet, it is difficult for fires to spread due to the low oxygen level.

468) Zimbabwe has the most official languages of any country; it has 16 official languages.

469) Alexander the Great, Julius Caesar, Genghis Khan, Napoleon, Mussolini, and Hitler all suffered from ailurophobia, a fear of cats.

470) A rhinoceros has three toes on each foot.

471) Rock paper scissors originated in China about 2,000 years ago.

472) The United States is collectively overweight by about 4 billion pounds.

473) Napoleon was attacked by rabbits and had to retreat. In 1807, Napoleon had just signed the Treaty of Tilsit, ending his war with Russia; to celebrate, he went on a rabbit hunt. Hundreds of rabbits had been gathered for the hunt in cages, but when they were released, they swarmed toward Napoleon and his men rather than running away. They swarmed Napoleon's legs and started climbing up him; he was forced to retreat to his coach and depart. Instead of wild rabbits, they had bought tame rabbits from farmers, so they weren't afraid of people and probably thought it was feeding time.

474) Only three people have died outside the earth's atmosphere; they were aboard *Soyuz 11* in 1971.

475) Horses have weak ciliary muscles that do a poor job of focusing their eyes, so they need to move their heads to adjust the focal length or angle of view until the image falls into view on a portion of their retina.

476) Ohio has the only non-rectangular state flag; it is a swallowtail shape.

477) Snickers is the world's best-selling candy bar.

478) There are 60 seconds in a minute and 360 degrees in a circle because the ancient Babylonians did math in base 60, instead of base 10, and developed the concepts.

479) Twenty-seven states are at least partly north of the southernmost point of Canada; Middle Island in Lake Erie is the most southern point

of Canada. It is approximately the latitude of Chicago which means that Alaska, California, Connecticut, Idaho, Illinois, Indiana, Iowa, Maine, Massachusetts, Michigan, Minnesota, Montana, Nebraska, Nevada, New Hampshire, New York, North Dakota, Ohio, Oregon, Pennsylvania, Rhode Island, South Dakota, Utah, Vermont, Washington, Wisconsin, and Wyoming are all at least partly north of Canada.

480) The busiest muscles in the human body are in the eyes; it is estimated that they move 100,000 times a day.

481) Four is the only number spelled out in English that has the same number of letters as its value.

482) Maine is the only state with a one-syllable name.

483) At up to 46 feet long, colossal squid are the largest invertebrate (no backbone) animal.

484) Napoleon wasn't short for his time. He was about 5 feet 7 inches; the average adult French male of his time was only 5 feet 5 inches, so he was taller than average. Some of the confusion is the units his height was reported in and that his guards, who he was usually seen with, were required to be quite tall.

485) The most used punctuation mark is the comma.

486) The opossum has the shortest known gestation period of any mammal, an average of just 12 days.

487) Water polo is the only sport where you can see teams defending goals of different sizes. The goal at the deep end is smaller than the goal at the shallow end. The inner sides of the goalposts are 10 feet apart; when the water depth is 5 feet or more, the crossbar is 3 feet from the water surface; when the water depth is less than 5 feet, the crossbar is 8 feet from the floor of the pool.

488) By volume, Tamu Massif is the world's largest volcano, either active or extinct; it is 1,000 miles east of Japan, under the Pacific Ocean, and is extinct.

489) Marie Curie is the only person to win Nobel Prizes in two different areas of science (physics and chemistry).

490) About 50% of human DNA is the same as a banana.

491) The cornea is the only part of the human body without a blood supply.

492) The Tibet region of China has the highest asphalt road in the world at 18,258 feet.

493) The world's largest gold depository is the Manhattan Federal Reserve Bank; it houses 7,700 tons of gold.

494) There are 88 constellations in the night sky.

495) Of all the senses, the sense of smell is most closely linked to memory.

496) La Paz, Bolivia, at an elevation of 11,942 feet, is the world's highest elevation national capital city.

497) Alaska is the longest state from north to south at 1,479 miles.

498) Alaska has 6,640 miles of coastline, more than the rest of the United States combined.

499) Honolulu has the only royal palace in the United States.

500) The giant and colossal squid have the largest eye of any animal; their eye is up to 11 inches in diameter.

501) The worldwide life expectancy at birth is 69 years.

502) A group of unicorns is called a blessing.

503) Alfred Carlton Gilbert, a 1908 Olympic gold medal pole vaulter, invented the Erector Set toy.

504) It only takes 23 people in a group to have a 50% chance that two will have the same birthday. This is known as the Birthday Paradox; with just 70 people, the probability goes up to 99.9%.

505) If uncoiled, the DNA in all cells of the human body would stretch about 10 billion miles.

506) Eight U.S. presidents were born as British subjects: George Washington, John Adams, Thomas Jefferson, James Madison, James Monroe, John Quincy Adams, Andrew Jackson, and William Henry Harrison.

507) The ZIP in ZIP Code stands for Zone Improvement Plan.

508) Canada's Wasaga Beach, on the shores of Lake Huron, is the world's longest freshwater beach; it is 14 miles long.

509) The harmonica is the world's best-selling musical instrument.

510) Arkansas has the only active diamond mine in the United States.

511) Petrichor is the word for the pleasant odor after a rain. Streptomyces bacteria in the soil produce a molecule called geosmin, which is released into the air when rain hits the ground producing the smell. Humans are extremely sensitive to the smell.

512) Australia has the lowest average elevation of any continent at 1,080 feet.

513) The average adult human heart pumps about 2,000 gallons of blood each day.

514) Your hearing is less sharp after you eat too much.

515) The Eskimo kiss of rubbing noses isn't really a kiss; it is called a kunik and is typically used as an expression of affection between an adult and a child. The Inuit kiss on the lips like many other cultures.

516) A group of owls is called a parliament.

517) *Pocahontas* was the first Disney animated film based on the life of a real person.

518) Of the 25 highest peaks in the world, 10 are in the Himalayas.

519) The story of Cinderella originated in China.

520) By volume, Lake Baikal, in Russia, is the largest freshwater lake in the world. It has a maximum depth of 5,387 feet and contains about 20% of the total unfrozen surface freshwater in the world.

521) The letter x begins the fewest words in the English language.

522) The world's most widely used vegetable is the onion.

523) Pirates wore earrings to improve their eyesight; they believed the precious metals in an earring had healing powers.

524) Rhinotillexomania is excessive nose picking.

525) About 24,000 people are killed worldwide by lightning each year.

526) The Statue of Liberty gets hit by lightning about 600 times per year.

527) The first published use of the word hello was in 1827. Hello is a relatively recent word and was initially used to attract attention or express surprise; it didn't get its current meaning until the telephone arrived.

528) At a cost of $160 billion, the International Space Station is the most expensive man-made object ever built.

529) Three countries are completely surrounded by one other country: Lesotho (surrounded by South Africa), and Vatican City and San Marino (both surrounded by Italy).

530) The longest English word with one syllable has nine letters; there are several words: scratched, screeched, stretched, straights, strengths, etc.

531) The bat is the only land mammal native to New Zealand.

532) Abraham Lincoln was the first president born outside the original 13 states.

533) By volume, the world's largest pyramid is in Mexico; the Great Pyramid of Cholula has a base of 450 meters on each side and a height of 66 meters.

534) There are about 6,900 living languages in the world. Just 6% of the languages account for 94% of the world's population. About half of the languages have fewer than 10,000 speakers, and one-quarter have fewer than 1,000 speakers.

535) Mercury and Venus are the only two planets in our solar system that don't have moons.

536) Five presidents regularly wore beards while in office: Abraham Lincoln, Ulysses S. Grant, Rutherford B. Hayes, James A. Garfield, and Benjamin Harrison.

537) Alaska is both the westernmost and easternmost state; parts of Alaska stretch into the Eastern Hemisphere.

538) Alligators are only naturally found in the United States and China.

539) By area, Great Salt Lake is the largest lake entirely within one state; it is 1,699 square miles.

540) Inspired by burrs, George de Mestral invented Velcro in the 1940s.

541) Mars is red because it is covered in iron oxide (rust).

542) Since the start of the Winter Olympics, five athletes have won medals at both the winter and summer games: Eddie Eagan (U.S.), Jacob Tullin Thams (Norway), Christa Luding-Rothenburger (East Germany), Clara Hughes (Canada), and Lauryn Williams (U.S.).

543) Checkers originated in Egypt as early as 200 BC.

544) The most perfectly-round, natural object known to man in the universe is a star 5,000 light-years away; before this discovery, the sun was the most perfectly-round, natural object known.

545) Scatomancy was popular in ancient Egypt; it is telling the future through someone's poop.

546) A group of rhinoceros is called a crash.

547) English is the official language of the most countries.

548) Today's British accent first appeared among the British upper class about the time of the American Revolution. Before that, the British accent was like Americans.

549) With 63.7 inches mean annual precipitation, Hawaii has the most rainfall of any state.

550) The video game company Nintendo was founded in 1889; it originally produced handmade playing cards.

551) The wheel was invented in about 3500 BC.

552) Frances Folsom Cleveland is the youngest U.S. first lady ever. She was 21 when she married Grover Cleveland in the White House; he was 49.

553) Teeth are the only part of the human body that cannot repair itself.

554) The Northern Hemisphere is warmer than the Southern Hemisphere by 1.5 degrees Celsius; it is due to ocean circulation.

555) At 37.8 degrees south latitude, Melbourne, Australia, is the southernmost city in the world with a population of over 1 million.

556) When the Persians were at war with the Egyptians, they rounded up and released as many cats as they could on the battlefield. Knowing the Egyptians reverence for cats, they knew they would not want to do anything to hurt the cats; the Persians won the battle.

557) Zero can't be represented in Roman numerals.

558) No witches were burned at the stake during the Salem witch trials; 20 were executed, but most were hung, and none were burned.

559) By area, New Mexico is 0.2% water, the lowest percentage of any state.

560) About 100 billion people have died in all of human history.

561) Bears have the best sense of smell of any land animal. Black bears have been observed to travel 18 miles in a straight line to a food source; grizzlies can find an elk carcass underwater, and polar bears can smell a seal through three feet of ice.

562) According to his wife, Abraham Lincoln's hobby was cats. He loved them and could play with them for hours; he once allowed a cat to eat from the table at a formal White House dinner.

563) The most used letter in the English alphabet is e.

564) Dogs were the first domesticated animal; they were domesticated up to 40,000 years ago.

565) In 1958 as a part of a junior high history class project, Robert Heft designed the current 50-star U.S. flag.

566) James is the most common first name of U.S. presidents: Madison, Monroe, Polk, Buchanan, Garfield, and Carter.

567) Polo is played on the largest field of any sport; the field is 300 yards by 160 yards.

568) A domestic cat shares 95.6% of its DNA with a tiger.

569) The tongue is the fastest healing part of the human body.

570) Equestrian and sailing are the only Olympic sports where men and women compete against each other.

571) A baby blue whale gains about 200 pounds of weight each day.

572) Roman gladiator fights started as a part of funerals; when wealthy nobles died, they would have bouts at the graveside.

573) Iceland has the highest per capita electricity consumption; it is about four times higher than in the United States.

574) Leprosy is probably the oldest known infectious disease in humans; its roots may stretch back millions of years.

575) Aluminum is the most abundant metal in the earth's crust.

576) Ulysses S. Grant was the first president to run against a woman candidate; Virginia Woodhull was a nominee of the Equal Rights Party in 1872.

577) In 2013, the remains of England's King Richard III were found buried under a parking lot in Leicester, England; in 1485, he was the last English king to die on the battlefield.

578) Collectively, the bacteria in an average human body weigh about four pounds.

579) According to the Bible, Goliath was six cubits tall, about nine feet.

580) Fireflies are a species of beetle.

581) The ancient Romans used human urine as a mouthwash; it was supposed to purge bacteria, and physicians claimed it whitened teeth and made them stronger. Upper-class women paid for bottled Portuguese urine since it was supposed to be the strongest on the continent.

582) The most common symbol on flags of the world is a star.

583) The Great Pyramid at Giza was the world's tallest man-made structure for over 3,800 years.

584) Indonesia has on average the shortest people in the world, an average of 5'2" for men and 4'10" for women.

585) In 1917, Janette Rankin, from Montana, became the first woman elected to the U.S. Congress.

586) Lake Maracaibo, Venezuela, has the most lightning strikes of any place in the world. Lightning storms occur for about 10 hours a night, 140 to 160 nights a year, for a total of about 1.2 million lightning discharges per year.

587) Oscar Zoroaster Phadrig Isaac Norman Henkle Emmannuel Ambroise Diggs is the real name of The Wizard of Oz.

588) In the song "Yankee Doodle," the term macaroni means stylish or fashionable. In late 18th century England, the term macaroni came to mean stylish or fashionable; in the song, it is used to mock the Americans, who think they can be stylish by simply sticking a feather in their cap.

589) The mangrove is the only tree that grows in saltwater.

590) Istanbul, Turkey, is the only major city in the world located on two continents, Europe and Asia.

591) Christ's name translated directly from Hebrew to English would be Joshua; Jesus comes about by translating Hebrew to Greek to Latin to English.

592) In average lawn or garden soil, a mole can dig 12-15 feet per hour.

593) Detroit is the only U.S. city to win three of the four major professional sports championships in the same year; in 1935, it won the NFL, NBA, and NHL championships.

594) Beetles are the most common group of insects. Flies are the second most common, and bees and ants are third.

595) Neil Armstrong didn't say, "one small step for man" when he set foot on the moon. He said, "one small step for a man"; that is what Armstrong claims he said, and audio analysis confirms it. It has been misquoted all these years.

596) Cleopatra was Greek.

597) Extant is the opposite of extinct.

598) Play-Doh was created as a wallpaper cleaning putty to remove coal dust in the 1930s.

599) Tsutomu Yamaguchi is the only recognized person in the world to survive both the Hiroshima and Nagasaki atomic bomb blasts. He was in Hiroshima on business for the first bomb and then returned home to Nagasaki.

600) Most of the world's supply of cork comes from cork oak trees, predominantly in Portugal and Spain.

# Facts 601-900

601) A human sneeze travels about 100 mph.

602) Birds don't urinate. They convert excess nitrogen to uric acid, instead of urea; it is less toxic and doesn't need to be diluted as much. It goes out with their other waste and saves water, so they don't have to drink as much.

603) At the first modern Olympics, silver medals were awarded to the winners; second place received bronze medals.

604) In Germany, you can't name your child Matti because it doesn't indicate gender; Germany has laws regarding the naming of children including that the name must indicate gender and must not negatively affect the child's well-being.

605) In his duty as a sheriff, President Grover Cleveland twice served as an executioner.

606) Montpelier, Vermont, is the only state capital without a McDonald's.

607) A polar bear's fur isn't white. It is transparent and appears white only because it reflects visible light.

608) The oceans are 71% of the earth's surface, but they only account for 0.02% of the earth's mass.

609) Owls have three eyelids; they have one for blinking, one for sleeping, and one for keeping their eyes clean.

610) At one point in the year, it is the same local time for people living in Oregon and Florida. A small part of eastern Oregon is in the Mountain Time Zone, and a small part of western Florida is in the Central Time Zone. When the change from daylight saving time to standard time is made, these two areas share the same time for one hour after the Central Time Zone has fallen back to standard time and before the Mountain Time Zone has.

611) The 2016 Rio de Janeiro Olympics was the first Summer Olympics held entirely during the winter. The other two Summer Olympics in the Southern Hemisphere had taken place at least partly in the spring.

612) Mongolia is the least densely populated country in the world; areas like Greenland have even lower density but aren't independent countries.

613) Antarctica is the windiest continent.

614) A catfish is the only animal that naturally has an odd number of whiskers.

615) Instead of 212 degrees Fahrenheit, the boiling point of water at the top of Mount Everest is about 160 degrees.

616) The arrector pili muscles, located near the root of human hair follicles, are responsible for goosebumps.

617) Up until 1954, traffic stop signs in the United States were yellow.

618) Over the last two centuries, each year has added about three months to average human life expectancy.

619) Southern Florida is the only place in the world that alligators and crocodiles exist together naturally in the wild.

620) Psychologist William Marston was one of the inventors of the polygraph and created the comics character Wonder Woman and her Lasso of Truth.

621) President Thomas Jefferson is commonly credited with inventing the swivel chair.

622) If the earth's history was condensed to 24 hours, humans would appear at 11:58:43 pm.

623) A crocodile can't stick its tongue out. It is attached to the roof of their mouth; their tongue helps keep their throat closed underwater, so they can open their mouth to hunt prey.

624) Before 1687, clocks didn't have minute hands.

625) Tuna need to swim continuously to breathe. They can't pump water through their gills without swimming.

626) A pirate yelling "Avast, ye mateys" is telling his mates to stop or cease.

627) Fruit flies were the very first animal to go into space. In 1947, they went up in a captured German V2 rocket; they were recovered alive.

628) A hippopotamus' skin is two inches thick; it is difficult for even bullets to penetrate it.

629) Cerebral hypoxia is the end cause of every human death. Lack of oxygen to the brain is the final cause of death, regardless of what initiates it.

630) A group of flamingos is called a flamboyance.

631) Sudan has more pyramids than any other country; it has almost twice as many as Egypt.

632) Thomas Jefferson had the largest personal book collection in the United States and sold it to become part of the Library of Congress after the library was destroyed in the War of 1812.

633) Orville Wright was the pilot in the first fatal airplane crash.

634) The United States doesn't have an official language.

635) Canada has more lakes than the rest of the world combined; it has more than 2 million lakes.

636) The Bible doesn't say how many wise men there were. It says wise men and mentions the gifts; there is no indication of how many wise men.

637) London didn't get back to its pre-WWII population until 2015.

638) Denmark's flag has lasted longer without change than any other country; it has been the same since at least 1370.

639) At 64 degrees north latitude, Reykjavik, Iceland, is the world's most northerly national capital city.

640) Of the 48 contiguous states, Olympia, Washington, is the most northern state capital.

641) Sea otters hold hands while they are sleeping, so they don't drift apart.

642) Washington is the most common place name in the United States.

643) China is the largest country with only one time zone; geographically, it has five time zones, but it chooses to use one standard time.

644) Twenty-two countries don't maintain an army; they include Andorra, Costa Rica, Panama, Grenada, Haiti, Iceland, and Liechtenstein.

645) Antarctica has the highest average elevation of any continent, an average of 8,200 feet.

646) On average, cats sleep 15 hours per day.

647) Antarctica is the driest continent; it only gets about eight inches of precipitation annually and is considered a desert.

648) If you drilled a hole straight through the center of the earth to the other side and jumped in, it would take 42 minutes to get to the other

side. You would accelerate until you got to the center and then decelerate until you got to the other side, where your speed would be zero again.

649) Louisa Adams and Melania Trump are the only two U.S. first ladies born outside the United States.

650) In 1888, the first vending machine in the United States dispensed Tutti-Frutti gum.

651) Built between 1825 and 1843, the world's first underwater tunnel was under London's Thames River.

652) Oregon has the only two-sided (different designs on each side) state flag.

653) Switzerland last went to war with another country in 1515.

654) On average, the Antarctic ice sheet is one mile thick.

655) The giraffe has the longest tail of any land animal; their tail can be up to eight feet long.

656) On *Sesame Street*, Big Bird is 8 feet 2 inches tall.

657) In its life, the sun has made about 20 orbits around the center of the Milky Way Galaxy.

658) Due to its unique chemical qualities, honey can remain edible for centuries; 3,000-year-old edible honey has been found in tombs.

659) Juneau, Alaska, is the least accessible state capital; you have to fly or take a boat.

660) Yuma, Arizona, is the sunniest city in the world; it averages 4,015 hours of sunshine annually, about 90% of daylight hours.

661) Roman gladiator bouts only resulted in death about 10 to 20% of the time. The bouts were generally not intended to be to the death; gladiators were expensive, and promoters didn't want to see them die needlessly.

662) In Greek mythology, they believed redheads turned into vampires when they died.

663) In your lifetime, your long-term memory can hold about 1 quadrillion bits of information.

664) Flamingos can only eat when their head is upside down.

665) Orlando, Florida, is the most visited U.S. city; New York City is second.

666) Limpet teeth are the strongest natural material known to man. Limpets are small, snail-like creatures; a single spaghetti strand of their teeth material could hold 3,300 pounds.

667) Time, person, and year are the three most used English nouns.

668) Eigengrau is the name for the dark gray color the eyes see in perfect darkness because of optic nerve signals.

669) Dragonflies may have the best vision of any animal. Humans have three light-sensitive proteins in the eye for red, blue, and green (trichromatic vision); dragonflies have up to 33. Their bulbous eyes have 30,000 facets and can see in all directions at once.

670) The brain is the highest percentage fat human organ. It is up to 60% fat, so everyone is a fathead.

671) In 1990, Benazir Bhutto of Pakistan was the first elected head of a nation to give birth in office.

672) At 7,000 feet, Santa Fe, New Mexico, is the highest elevation state capital.

673) By area, Ukraine is the largest country entirely in Europe; it is 223,000 square miles.

674) A polar bear's skin is black.

675) The pizza served in the United States each day would cover an area of about 100 acres.

676) Most birds lack a sense of smell.

677) Oysters can change their gender based on environmental conditions; they are born male but can change back and forth based on conditions.

678) The Challenger Deep is the deepest known location in the oceans; it is in the Mariana Trench, in the Pacific Ocean, and is 36,070 feet deep.

679) Octopus blood is blue. It contains a copper-rich protein that carries oxygen instead of the iron-rich protein in other animals.

680) At 41 degrees south latitude, Wellington, New Zealand, is the world's most southerly national capital.

681) Rats can't vomit; this makes them particularly vulnerable to poison.

682) The Eiffel Tower was originally intended for Barcelona; Spain rejected the project.

683) Nebraska has the most miles of rivers of any state; it has four major rivers: Platte, Niobrara, Missouri, and Republican.

684) An average adult English speaker has 20,000 words in their vocabulary.

685) The ancient Romans used human urine to wash clothes.

686) South Africa has three national capital cities. Pretoria is the administrative capital; Cape Town is the legislative capital, and Bloemfontein is the judicial capital.

687) The praying mantis is the only insect that can turn its head.

688) Miami is the only major U.S. city founded by a woman; Julia Tuttle was a businesswoman and the original owner of the land upon which Miami was built.

689) Based on the number of participants, soccer is the most popular sport in the world; badminton is second, and field hockey is third.

690) There are no landlocked countries in North America.

691) La Rinconada, Peru, is the world's highest elevation city; it is a mining town at 16,700 feet and has about 30,000 residents.

692) The Hundred Years War between England and France lasted 116 years, from 1337 to 1453.

693) Regarding letters, the terms uppercase and lowercase originated in early print shops. The individual pieces of metal type were kept in boxes called cases; the smaller, more frequently used letters were kept in a lower case that was easier to reach; the less frequently used capital letters were kept in an upper case.

694) The sun accounts for 99.8% of our solar system's total mass.

695) The moon and sun fit together so perfectly in a solar eclipse because the sun is about 400 times larger than the moon, and it is also about 400 times further away from the earth, so the two appear to be the same size in the sky.

696) Sunsets on Mars are blue.

697) The sooty shearwater has the world's longest distance migration. It is a common seabird and has been tracked electronically migrating 40,000 miles.

698) In the human body, a limbal dermoid is a cyst in the eye, formed in the womb when skin cells get misplaced in the eye; the cyst can grow hair, cartilage, sweat glands, and even teeth.

699) At 100 pounds, James Madison was the lightest president.

700) Based on land area, Hulunbuir, China, is the largest city in the world; it is 102,000 square miles, about the size of Colorado.

701) Europe is the only continent without a significant desert.

702) The Congo is the only river that crosses the equator in both a northerly and southerly direction.

703) The earliest known reference to a vending machine is in 1st century Egypt. It dispensed holy water; when a coin was deposited, it fell on a pan that was attached to a lever. The lever opened a valve that let some water flow out. The pan continued to tilt with the weight of the coin until it fell off, and a counterweight snapped the lever up and turned off the valve.

704) A pangram is a sentence or verse that contains all letters in the alphabet at least once, such as "The quick brown fox jumps over a lazy dog."

705) Search engines can access about 0.03% of the internet. About 99.96% of the internet is the deep web, which is anything that is password-protected, requires filling out a form, etc. such as email, social media profiles, databases, etc. The tiny remaining portion is the dark web, which is a subset of the deep web and is encrypted for illegal or secretive purposes.

706) While in the White House, Calvin Coolidge had a pet raccoon; the raccoon was a gift and was supposed to be served for Thanksgiving dinner. Coolidge made it a pet and even walked it on a leash on the White House grounds.

707) Bangkok, Thailand, is the most visited city in the world; London is second.

708) Andrew Jackson is the only president held as a prisoner of war; he joined the Revolutionary War at age 13 and was captured by the British.

709) Iceland has the oldest parliament in the world; it has existed since 930 AD.

710) Alaska is the only state name that can be typed on one row of a standard keyboard.

711) Eighty percent of all the paragraphs written in English contain the word "the."

712) To mourn the deaths of their cats, ancient Egyptians shaved off their eyebrows.

713) The giant armadillo has the most teeth (up to 100) of any land animal.

714) Bananas are the most frequently sold item at Walmart.

715) A giraffe has the highest blood pressure of any animal; it is about 300 over 200.

716) The 1883 eruption of Krakatoa is the loudest sound in recorded history; it ruptured people's eardrums 40 miles away and was clearly heard 3,000 miles away.

717) Giraffes need the least sleep of any mammal; on average, they only sleep 30 minutes a day, just a few minutes at a time.

718) W is the shortest three-syllable word in English. The letters of the alphabet are generally also considered words since they are nouns referring to the letter.

719) Amen is in 1,200 different languages, without change.

720) Sulfur gives onions their distinctive smell; when cut or crushed, a chemical reaction changes an amino acid into a sulfur compound.

721) On average, the Netherlands has the tallest people in the world, with an average of 5'11 1/2" for men and 5'6 1/2" for women.

722) The Red Sea is the world's warmest sea.

723) At 19,341 feet, Mount Kilimanjaro is the world's highest mountain that isn't part of a range.

724) At 6'4", Abraham Lincoln was the tallest U.S. president.

725) The stapes, in the middle ear, is the smallest bone in the human body.

726) At 5,000 years old, the bristlecone pine species is the oldest living individual tree.

727) There are about 10 times more bacterial cells in the human body than there are body cells.

728) The probability that any single glass of water contains at least one molecule of water drunk by Cleopatra is almost 100%. There are about 1,000 times as many molecules of water in a glass as there are glasses of water in the earth's water supply. If water molecules spread through the entire water supply, any given glass of water should contain 1,000 molecules of water from any other glass.

729) Spain kept the discovery of chocolate a national secret for nearly a century.

730) The closest living relative to the Tyrannosaurus Rex is the chicken.

731) The Wall Street area in New York City is named after a barrier built by the Dutch in the 17th century to protect against Indian attacks.

732) Based on their global following, soccer is the most popular sport in the world; cricket is second; field hockey is third.

733) Rodents have more species than any other mammal.

734) A moth grub moving inside the bean causes a jumping bean to jump.

735) The United States has more tornadoes than any other country.

736) The Tour de France bicycle race has the most in-person spectators of any single sporting event in the world. It attracts 12 to 15 million spectators.

737) Theodore Roosevelt was the first American to win a Nobel Prize of any kind. He won the 1906 Peace Prize; the Nobel Prizes started in 1901.

738) Apples, peaches, and raspberries belong to the rose plant family.

739) Bird's nest soup is made from the nests of swifts; the nest is saliva that has dried and hardened.

740) Australia is the only continent without glaciers.

741) Austin, Texas, is the largest population city in the United States that doesn't have an MLB, NFL, NBA, or NHL team; it is the 11th largest city in the United States.

742) The hard piece at the end of a shoelace is called an aglet.

743) Of the seven wonders of the ancient world, only the Great Pyramid of Giza still exists. The Lighthouse at Alexandria was the last wonder to disappear; it was toppled by earthquakes in the early 14th century, and its ruined stones were carried off by the late 15th century.

744) The Nile crocodile has the greatest bite force of any animal; it can bite down with 5,000 psi.

745) The monkeys Mizaru, Kikazaru, and Iwazaru are better known as see no evil, hear no evil, and speak no evil.

746) When you die, hearing is the last sense to go.

747) The sperm whale has the largest brain of any animal. Compared to about 3 pounds for a human brain, a sperm whale's brain is about 17 pounds.

748) At age 32, Sally Ride is the youngest American astronaut in space.

749) Australia is the only continent without an active volcano.

750) A normal house cat has 18 claws; there are five on each front paw and four on each back paw.

751) Dating back to the 6th century, the pretzel is the world's oldest snack food.

752) The moon is moving away from the earth by about 1.5 inches per year.

753) Four U.S. presidents have won the Nobel Peace Prize: Theodore Roosevelt, Woodrow Wilson, Jimmy Carter, and Barack Obama.

754) Santa Fe, New Mexico, is the only two-word state capital in a two-word state.

755) The United States has the most dogs of any country in the world; Brazil has the second most.

756) Rio de Janeiro, Brazil, was the only European capital outside of Europe; it was the capital of Portugal from 1808 to 1822. Napoleon was invading Portugal at the time, so the Portuguese royal family moved to Rio, and it became the capital.

757) At its closest point, the distance between the United States and Russia is 2.4 miles.

758) Human babies have 300 bones; some fuse together to form the 206 bones in adults.

759) By 70 years of age, the average person will have shed 105 pounds of skin.

760) You would swim the same speed through syrup as you do through water; the additional drag is canceled out by the additional force generated from each stroke.

761) Thirty-five percent of the world's population drives on the left side.

762) Of the 48 contiguous states, Austin, Texas, is the most southern state capital.

763) Delaware has the lowest average elevation of any state, just 60 feet.

764) During WWII when Hitler visited Paris, the French cut the Eiffel Tower lift cables, so Hitler would have to climb the steps if he wanted to go to the top.

765) After watching workers move timber, Frank Lloyd Wright's son John invented Lincoln Logs.

766) Phidipedes ran the first marathon upon which all others are based. He ran 140 miles round trip from Athens to Sparta over mountain terrain to ask for military aid, marched 26 miles from Athens to Marathon, fought all morning, and then ran 26 miles to Athens with the victory news and died of exhaustion.

767) Thomas Edison is credited with suggesting the word hello be used when answering a telephone; Alexander Graham Bell thought ahoy was better.

768) There are 45 miles of nerves in the human body.

769) The Twinkie filling flavor was originally banana cream.

770) With three counties, Delaware has the fewest counties of any state.

771) There are 293 possible ways to make change for a dollar.

772) Venus has a longer day than its year. It takes 243 days for one rotation (1 day) and 225 days for one orbit around the sun (1 year).

773) Chang is the most common surname in the world.

774) Only the nine-banded armadillo and humans are known to be infected with leprosy.

775) The company Google was originally called Backrub.

776) The British pound is the world's oldest currency still in use; it is 1,200 years old.

777) Many U.S. police departments adopted navy blue uniforms because they were surplus army uniforms from the Civil War.

778) On April 23, 2005, the first video ever uploaded to YouTube was *Meet Me at the Zoo*. It was 19 seconds of a boy explaining that elephants have long tusks.

779) Blind people still dream. People who were born blind or lost their sight at four to five years old or younger don't have visual imagery in their dreams, but people who lost their sight later in life continue to dream with visual imagery.

780) Instead of the five tastes (sweet, savory, sour, bitter, and salty) that humans can detect, whales and dolphins can only taste salty.

781) The Chinese giant salamander is the largest amphibian in the world and can grow to lengths of almost six feet.

782) In traditional vampire folklore, one of their weaknesses is arithmomania, a compulsion to count things. This weakness can be used to defend against them by placing grains of rice or sand out, which they will be compelled to count. Therefore, *Sesame Street's* Count von Count's love of counting is part of being a vampire.

783) Hippos don't really swim; they walk underwater. If they are submerged, they don't swim back to the surface; they just walk on the bottom until they reach shallower water. They can hold their breath for five minutes or longer.

784) Goats can develop accents. Researchers found that a goat's accent changed as they aged and moved in different groups; this disproves the idea that their voices are entirely genetic and suggests that most mammals can develop an accent from their surroundings.

785) Despite having by far the longest coastline of any country in the world, the Royal Canadian Navy only has about 36 ships.

786) The Declaration of Independence wasn't signed on July 4, 1776. It was signed on August 2, 1776; it was adopted by Congress on July 4, 1776.

787) If you complete courses in archery, pistol shooting, sailing, and fencing at the Massachusetts Institute of Technology, you can be recognized as a certified pirate.

788) Your fingernails grow 2-3 times faster than your toenails, and the fingernails on your dominant hand tend to grow faster than on your other hand.

789) Abel Tasman discovered Tasmania, New Zealand, and Fiji on his first voyage, but he completely missed Australia.

790) The burnt part of a candlewick is called the snaste.

791) Almost 1% of the world's population eats at McDonald's each day.

792) Jellyfish are the oldest multi-organ animals in the world. They evolved 550 million years ago and have no brain or nervous system, and their body is 90% water.

793) The loop on a belt that keeps the end in place after it has passed through the buckle is called the keeper.

794) Only about 2% of the islands in the Caribbean are inhabited.

795) Cicadas are the world's loudest insects. They can reach about 120 decibels, which is equivalent to sitting in the front row of a loud rock concert.

796) A group of pandas is called an embarrassment.

797) Through nuclear fusion, the sun loses about 4.3 million tons of mass per second as it is transformed into energy.

798) We won't always have the same North Star. In 13,000 years, Polaris, the current North Star, will be replaced by Vega, and 26,000 years from now, Polaris will be back as the North Star. This is because of a change in the direction of the earth's axis due to a motion called precession. If you think of a spinning top given a slight nudge, the top traces out a cone pattern; that is how the earth moves on its axis. The earth bulges out at the equator, and the gravitational attraction of the moon and sun on the bulge causes the precession, which repeats in a 26,000-year cycle.

799) About 90% of the coal we burn today came about because wood-eating bacteria didn't evolve until about 60 million years after trees existed. For tens of millions of years, all the dead tree material remained intact; trees would fall on top of each other, and the weight of the wood compressed the trees into peat and then into coal. Had wood-eating bacteria been around, they would have broken the carbon bonds and released carbon and oxygen into the air; instead, the carbon remained in the wood. Adding to the coal formation, early trees were tall, up to 160 feet, with thin trunks, fernlike leaves on top, and very shallow roots, so they fell over very easily. This era from 359 to 299 million years ago is known as the Carboniferous Period because of the large amounts of coal formed.

800) Scientists believe that human fingers and toes prune in water due to an evolutionary adaptation. The wrinkles in the skin improve your grip on wet or submerged objects, channeling away water like rain treads on car tires.

801) Despite deaths and injuries, staged train collisions were a spectator attraction from 1896 up until the Great Depression. In 1896, Crush, Texas, was a temporary site established for a one-day publicity stunt of a staged train wreck. It was organized by William George Crush, general passenger agent of the Missouri-Kansas-Texas Railroad. No admission was charged, but the railway charged $2 for every round-trip to get to the site, which also had a restaurant, midway, and medicine show. An estimated 40,000 people attended. For the main event, two unmanned six-car trains crashed into each other at 50 mph. Despite what mechanics had assured, the steam boilers on both trains exploded, creating flying debris that killed two people and injured many others. The spectators had been required to observe the collision from a hill 200 yards away, but they still weren't safe from

the flying wood and metal. The staged collisions became popular, and Scott Joplin even wrote the "Great Crush Collision March."

802) Recent research suggests that ice is slippery because there are loose water molecules on the surface that essentially act like marbles on a floor. Prior theories that it was due to pressure creating a thin layer of water on the surface have been disproven since the pressure would have to be far too great.

803) A female octopus can lay tens of thousands of eggs at one time, and when they hatch, she dies. She reproduces only once, and after she lays her eggs, she doesn't eat and puts all her energy into caring for them.

804) Camels store water in their bloodstream, not in their hump; they can drink up to 20 gallons at a time. The hump is almost all fat and serves as an alternative energy source and helps regulate body temperature. By concentrating fat in the hump instead of being spread over their body, they are better able to handle hot climates.

805) Due to lava flows from the Kilauea volcano, the Big Island of Hawaii is getting 42 acres larger each year.

806) The three-line symbol you typically find in the upper corner of a screen that you click or tap to get to a menu is called the hamburger button because it looks like a hamburger.

807) Saudi Arabia imports camels and sand from Australia. Camels are a large part of the Muslim diet and are in short supply in Saudi Arabia, so they import camels from Australia, which has the world's largest wild camel population. Saudi Arabia also imports Australia's garnet sand because its unique properties make it ideal for sandblasting.

808) If you fly directly south from Detroit, Michigan, you will hit Canada. You will fly over Windsor, Ontario, before re-entering the United States.

809) Up through the Victorian era, it was common for both boys and girls to wear dresses until the age of seven. Boys wore dresses primarily for practical reasons; dressing and potty training were easier, and dresses weren't as easily outgrown.

810) During WWII, Tootsie Rolls were part of soldier rations; they were durable in all weather conditions and were good for quick energy.

811) President Rutherford B. Hayes was the first American to own a Siamese cat. The cat was a gift to the president and first lady from the American consul in Bangkok.

812) Up until a 1747 proclamation by Spain's King Ferdinand VI, many Europeans believed California was an island. The misconception started in 1510 when Spanish novelist Garci Rodríguez de Montalvo wrote *Las Sergas de Esplandián*, about a mythical island called California. His work formed the basis for naming California, and the name propagated the idea that it was an island.

813) President James Garfield could simultaneously write in Greek with one hand and Latin with the other. He was ambidextrous and taught both languages while attending college.

814) If you smoothed out all the wrinkles in your brain, it would lie flat about the size of a pillowcase.

815) Since the origin of humans, the sun has only finished 1/1250th of an orbit around the center of the Milky Way Galaxy.

816) There are more insects in one square mile of empty field than there are people in the world.

817) In medieval manuscripts, it is common to see pictures of knights fighting snails; no one knows why.

818) There are at least 24 dialects of English spoken in the United States.

819) Worker ants, the most common and smallest ants in any colony who do most of the work, are all sterile females.

820) Rascette lines are the creases on your inner wrist.

821) In Victorian times, photography subjects were encouraged to say "prunes" instead of "cheese." Among other reasons, Victorians thought it was classless to show a big toothy smile.

822) Gold is so malleable that you could create a wire one micron thick that would stretch around the world with just 20 ounces of gold. One ounce, about the size of a quarter, can be beaten into a continuous 100-square-foot sheet.

823) The ketchup used by McDonald's annually would fill 50 Olympic size swimming pools.

824) In 1916, four years before women were given the right to vote, the first woman was elected to the U.S. Congress.

825) Written out in English, eight billion is the second number alphabetically, no matter how high you go.

826) Wilmer McLean's homes were involved in both the beginning and end of the American Civil War. On July 21, 1861, the First Battle of Bull

Run took place on his farm near Manassas, Virginia. Afterward, he moved to Appomattox, Virginia, to escape the war, but in 1865, General Robert E. Lee surrendered to Ulysses S. Grant in McLean's house in Appomattox.

827) Eighteen countries don't have any natural rivers: Bahamas, Bahrain, Comoros, Kiribati, Kuwait, Maldives, Malta, Marshall Islands, Monaco, Nauru, Oman, Qatar, Saudi Arabia, Tonga, Tuvalu, United Arab Emirates, Vatican City, and Yemen.

828) Alaska has all five of the largest land area cities in the United States: Yakutat, Sitka, Juneau, Wrangell, and Anchorage.

829) Bombardier beetles have a unique defense mechanism; they emit a hot noxious chemical spray that is produced from a reaction between hydroquinone and hydrogen peroxide, which are stored in two reservoirs in the beetle's abdomen. When the solutions are mixed with catalysts, the heat from the reaction brings the mixture to near the boiling point of water and produces gas that drives the ejection. The spray can be fatal to attacking insects. There are over 500 species of bombardier beetles, and they live on all continents except Antarctica.

830) The Pacific Ocean is so large that at some points it is antipodal to itself. Two points are antipodal if they are on diametrically opposite sides of the earth. At some points in the Pacific Ocean, you could go straight through the center of the earth and come out on the other side and still be in the Pacific Ocean.

831) In 1943, the Slinky was invented by accident by Richard James, a mechanical engineer. He was devising springs that could keep sensitive ship equipment steady at sea, and after accidentally knocking some samples off a shelf, he watched as the spring righted itself.

832) Dogs aren't colorblind, but they only have 20% of the cone photoreceptor cells that control color perception that humans have. Dogs see in shades of yellow and blue and cannot see the range of colors from green to red, so dogs see the colors of the world as basically yellow, blue, and gray.

833) Measured by its share of the world's population, the largest empire in history was the Persian Empire, which accounted for approximately 44% of the world's population in 480 BC. In contrast, the British Empire accounted for about 23% of the world's population at its peak.

834) The earth weighs about 13,170,000,000,000,000,000,000,000 pounds.

835) Clouds appear to be darker because they are thicker, which prevents more light from passing through; thinner clouds allow more light through and appear white. Seen from an airplane, the top of the cloud will still appear white since the top receives more light. As water droplets and ice crystals in a cloud thicken when it is about to rain, they scatter much less light, and the cloud appears almost black.

836) Riding a wave upstream on the Amazon River, people have surfed for 8 miles and over 30 minutes continuously. The Pororoca is a tidal bore wave; it is up to 13 feet high, travels up to 500 miles inland upstream, and has become popular with surfers. The wave occurs during new and full moons when the ocean tide is the highest and water flows in from the Atlantic. The phenomenon is most pronounced during the spring equinox in March when the moon and sun are in direct alignment with the earth and their gravitational pull is combined. As it moves upriver, the wave can be quite destructive, and the water is filled with debris.

837) A penny dropped from the 1,250-foot Empire State Building wouldn't kill a bystander below. Due to air resistance, the penny would reach its maximum speed after falling only about 50 feet. When it reached the ground, it would only be moving 25 mph, enough to hurt but nowhere near enough to kill.

838) Frozen seawater contains about one-tenth of the salt content found in liquid seawater because most of the salt separates from the water as it freezes. Due to its salt content, seawater freezes at about 28.4 degrees Fahrenheit.

839) In 18th century England, pineapples were so rare and such a status symbol that a single pineapple could sell for the equivalent of $8,000 today. You could even rent a pineapple for the evening to show off to guests.

840) On the animated television show *The Simpsons*, only God and Jesus have five fingers; all other characters have four.

841) When multiple story apartments were first built, the rich lived on the ground floor and not on the upper floors. When the Romans first built 9-10 story apartment buildings, wealthier people lived on ground floors since higher floors wouldn't typically have running water or bathrooms and required climbing up multiple flights of stairs. It wasn't until the elevator came about in the latter 1800s that upper floors became status symbols.

842) By area, Vatican City is the smallest country in the world; it is so small that there are 5.88 popes per square mile, with just the current pope.

843) A strawberry isn't a berry, but a banana is. Botanically, a berry must have three layers: a protective outer layer, a fleshy middle, and an inner part that holds the seeds. It must also have two or more seeds and come from a flower with only one ovary. Strawberries come from a single flower with more than one ovary, making them an aggregate fruit. True berries come from one flower with one ovary and typically have several seeds.

844) Reaching only about two feet in length, the cookiecutter shark's name comes from its unusual feeding method; it gouges out round plugs of flesh from larger animals.

845) The smallest thing ever photographed is the shadow of a single atom. In 2012, scientists were able to take a picture of the shadow produced by a single atom. Using an electrical field, they suspended the atom in a vacuum chamber and shot a laser beam at it to produce the shadow.

846) Modern humans appeared about 200,000 years ago, but recorded history only dates back about 5,000 years, so about 97.5% of human history is unrecorded.

847) Only about 8% of the world's currency exists as physical cash; the rest is in electronic accounts.

848) Humans have explored only about 5% of the ocean floor.

849) Cats have 32 muscles in each ear and can move each ear independently. To locate sounds, they can also swivel and rotate their ears 180 degrees. Humans have 6 muscles in each ear.

850) Boston and Austin are the only two U.S. state capitals with rhyming names.

851) At up to 19 feet long, the king cobra is the largest venomous snake.

852) Your purlicue is the skin connecting your fingers and thumb.

853) Cats have fallen from heights as great as 32 stories and survived. The cat that fell 32 stories had a chipped tooth and collapsed lung but went home two days after the fall. Researchers believe that cats instinctively know how to fall; for shorter falls up to about seven stories, cats don't reach terminal velocity and try to land feet first. For higher falls above seven stories where they reach terminal velocity, they splay their limbs out like a parachute and land on their belly,

increasing the chance of a collapsed lung or broken rib but greatly reducing the chance of a broken leg.

854) In 1845, Portland, Oregon, got its name when Asa Lovejoy and Francis Pettygrove flipped a coin. Lovejoy was from Massachusetts and wanted to name the new settlement Boston; Pettygrove was from Maine and wanted to name the new town Portland.

855) In the 13th century, Pope Gregory IX believed that black cats were an instrument of Satan; he condemned cats across Europe, and they were hunted down and killed.

856) At up to 10 feet long and 250 pounds, the Komodo dragon is the largest lizard in the world.

857) At its peak, the Roman Empire was about 2.5 million square miles, making it only the 19th largest empire by area in history.

858) The banana is the world's largest herb plant, with species growing up to 100 feet tall; it doesn't have a true woody trunk like a tree and behaves like a perennial.

859) In old age, human brains shrink by 10-15%; whereas, chimpanzees, our closest primate relatives, show no brain shrinkage with age. Researchers believe it may be due to extended longevity in humans that brain evolution hasn't kept up with.

860) A desert locust swarm can cover 460 square miles and contain billions of locusts that can eat their weight in plants each day, consuming potentially hundreds of millions of pounds of vegetation per day.

861) Because of its very high salt content, it is almost impossible for a human to drown in the Dead Sea. A human body can't sink, but drownings have occurred when someone gets stuck on their stomach and can't get turned over. Experts recommend spending no more than 20 minutes at a time in the water, to avoid dehydration and electrolyte imbalance from the high salt content.

862) Dire wolves, as seen in *Game of Thrones*, existed in the Americas up to about 10,000 years ago. They were about the same size as the largest modern gray wolves, at about 150 pounds on average, but their teeth were larger and had greater shearing ability. They also had the highest bite force of any known Canis species.

863) Almost the entire continent of South America is east of the easternmost point of Florida. Mainland South America and Florida only overlap for a little more than one degree of longitude.

864) Despite her family ruling Egypt for about 270 years before her reign, Cleopatra was the first in her family to learn Egyptian.

865) If you wrote out every number in English (one, two, three, etc.), you wouldn't use the letter b until you reached one billion.

866) Nebraska is the only state that is at least three states or provinces away from the ocean in every direction.

867) Through a process called REM atonia, people don't sneeze while they sleep because the brain shuts down the reflexes that would result in a sneeze.

868) The common cold likely came from camels. Researchers have found that along with being the source of the Middle East Respiratory Syndrome (MERS) virus, camels are the likely source of the common cold that spread to humans thousands of years ago.

869) Unwinding a roll of Scotch tape can produce enough x-rays to image a finger. As the tape is unpeeled and its adhesive snaps free of the surface, flows of electrons are released. The electrical currents generate strong, short bursts of x-rays, each about one billionth of a second long containing about 300,000 x-ray photons. Scientists were able to use the x-rays to image a finger. However, the phenomenon has been observed only when the tape is unpeeled in a vacuum.

870) Canada has more area devoted to national parks than any other country. There are over 145,000 square miles of national parks, an area larger than Norway.

871) In Michigan, you are never more than six miles from a body of water. Michigan has over 11,000 inland lakes plus four of the five Great Lakes.

872) The practice of using BC and AD for years wasn't established until the 6th century.

873) The sound of pain around the world differs. English speakers typically say "ouch!" or "aww!"; Spanish speakers usually say "uy!" or "ay!"; French speakers say "aïe!"; Germans say "aua!" or "autsch!"; Russians say "oi!"

874) Before electricity and gas lamps, it was common for people to wake in the middle of the night, splitting their sleep into two periods. People would engage in different activities when they woke and then go back to sleep. People went to bed much earlier, and there was no prestige or value placed on staying up late by candlelight; even the wealthy, who could afford candlelight, felt there were better ways to spend their money.

875) A rat's front teeth grow 4½ to 5½ inches each year; like other rodents, they wear them down gnawing.

876) Only one side of the moon is visible from the earth because the moon rotates on its axis at the same rate that it orbits the earth, which is known as synchronous rotation or tidal locking.

877) In the wild, there is no such thing as an alpha male wolf. Wolves act like families, with older members as leaders, so the leaders are simply parents. There's no fighting to move up the hierarchy, and they aren't born as leaders or followers.

878) The manchineel tree, which is native to tropical southern North America and northern South America, is extremely toxic in all forms. Its milky white sap contains skin irritants that can cause blistering, even from standing beneath the tree during rain. Burning the tree can cause eye injuries, and the fruit is possibly fatal, producing internal bleeding.

879) Studies have shown that the shape of an animal's eye pupil are evolutionary adaptations based on whether it's a predator or prey and how low to the ground the animal is. Circular pupils tend to belong to predators; rectangular pupils belong to grazing prey and provide a wider field of vision to see predators. Rectangular pupils also allow more light in without absorbing too much light from above the head, so grazing animals can see the grass and their surroundings better. For predators, the proximity to the ground seems to dictate whether an animal has round or vertical pupils. Vertical pupils, like snakes and small cats, can expand much more than round pupils and provide more light for nocturnal activity and greater depth perception. The advantages diminish as the animal gets further away from the ground; this may be why larger cats and humans have round pupils.

880) The Meganeura is the largest known flying insect to ever exist. It lived more than 300 million years ago and was a dragonfly-like insect that had a wingspan of about 2.5 feet. It was a carnivore and fed on other insects and small amphibians.

881) About 82% of the world's population has never flown on an airplane.

882) Mosquitos don't have teeth, but a mosquito's proboscis has 47 sharp edges on its tip that help it cut through skin and even clothing. The pain you feel from a mosquito bite is from the initial stab of sticking its proboscis into you.

883) A tornado can be nearly invisible. Since a tornado is just made up of wind, you don't see the tornado; what you see are the water droplets, dust, and debris that it picks up.

884) Manatees are tropical animals and can suffer from cold stress if water temperatures fall below 68 degrees Fahrenheit.

885) The Statue of Liberty is made of copper; about 62,000 pounds of copper were used to create it, and it looked like a new penny when it was first created.

886) Insects only have one blood vessel; they have a single tube with the heart at one end and the aorta at the other that pumps blood to the brain. The blood flows back and fills all the spaces in the insect's body, so all the internal organs are floating in blood.

887) Dogs stare at you when they poop because they know they are vulnerable at that time, and they are looking to you, a member of their pack, for protection.

888) President John Quincy Adams believed that the earth was hollow and signed off on an expedition to explore the empty core; the expedition never took place.

889) Snails are almost completely blind and don't have any mechanism to hear either, but their sense of smell is extraordinary.

890) An adult blue whale's stomach can hold 2,200 pounds of krill at a time, and they require almost 9,000 pounds of krill a day.

891) Moray eels have two pairs of jaws. They have strong flesh-tearing primary jaws that can cut through bone, and they have a pharyngeal jaw, a second pair of jaws located in their throat. When the eel captures prey with its primary jaws, it can use its secondary pharyngeal jaws to grab the prey and drag it down into its gullet for easy swallowing.

892) Oxford University existed about 350 years before the start of the Inca and Aztec empires. There was teaching at Oxford as early as 1076, making it the third-oldest university in continuous operation in the world and the oldest English-speaking university. The Aztec and Incan empires weren't founded until the 1430s.

893) The United States borders three oceans: the Atlantic, Pacific, and the Arctic. Alaska's northern border is on the Arctic Ocean.

894) Sand dunes cover only about 15% of the Sahara Desert; rock plateaus and coarse gravel cover the majority.

895) It does snow occasionally in the Sahara Desert. There have been three recorded episodes of significant snowfall: February 1979, December 2016, and January 2018.

896) There are about 10,000 stars in the known universe for every grain of sand on the earth.

897) Human stomach acid is about as strong as battery acid and capable of destroying metal. Gastric acid consists of potassium chloride, sodium chloride, and hydrochloric acid, and on a PH scale of 0-14 with 0 being the most acidic and 7 being neutral, it typically measures between 1 and 3.

898) Demodex mites live on your face, and you are more likely to have them the older you get. The largest is about one-third of a millimeter long, and they are sausage-shaped, with eight legs clustered in their front third. They spend most of their time buried head down in your hair follicles; they are mostly found in our eyelids, nose, cheeks, forehead, and chin. They like areas that have a lot of oils, which is why they prefer the face. They can leave the hair follicles and slowly walk around on the skin, especially at night as they try to avoid light. The mites are transferred from person to person through contact with hair, eyebrows, and the sebaceous glands of the face. They eat, crawl, and reproduce on your face; the entire cycle from reproduction through death is about two weeks.

899) The average garden snail has over 14,000 teeth that are arranged in rows on their tongue. The typical snail tongue might have 120 rows of 100 teeth; some species have more than 20,000 teeth.

900) The gender of most turtles, alligators, and crocodiles is determined after fertilization. The temperature of the eggs decides whether the offspring will be male or female; this is called temperature-dependent sex determination.

# Facts 901-1200

901) The Easter Island statues have full bodies, not just heads. The remainder of the body is buried; the tallest statue excavated is 33 feet high.

902) Outer space smells most like the burning odor of hydrocarbons; astronauts have reported smelling burned or fried steak after a spacewalk.

903) Sharks have been around longer than trees. The first sharks appeared about 450 million years ago; the first trees appeared about 385 million years ago.

904) Dunce caps originally were a sign of intelligence. Thirteenth-century philosopher John Duns Scotus created the idea of the pointy hat as a reverse funnel to spread knowledge into the brain; the hats became popular and a symbol of high intelligence. In the 1500s, Scotus' ideas fell out of favor, and the pointy hat eventually came to mean the opposite.

905) If you are locked in a completely sealed room, you will die from carbon dioxide poisoning before you die from lack of oxygen.

906) At 8.1 square miles, Nauru, in the South Pacific, is the smallest island country.

907) Phosphenes are the rings or spots of light you see when you rub your eyes.

908) Murmurations are the patterns starlings create when they flock together in the sky in swooping coordinated patterns.

909) Cats can drink saltwater and stay hydrated. Their kidneys are efficient enough to filter out the salt and use the water.

910) Humans are the only animals with chins; scientists don't know why.

911) The toy company Mattel originally sold picture frames and later dollhouse furniture.

912) To make it easier to give birth, hammerhead sharks are born with soft hammers bent back toward the tail.

913) Strengths is the longest word in the English language with only one vowel.

914) Hawaii essentially has its own time zone. It is in the Hawaii-Aleutian Time Zone that includes Hawaii and Alaska's Aleutian Islands west of 169° 30' W longitude.

915) Dogs usually use their right ear when listening to other dogs, but they use their left ear when they hear threatening sounds.

916) On average, a U.S. dollar bill only lasts about 18 months before it needs to be taken out of circulation and replaced.

917) The first video game console was the 1972 Magnavox Odyssey. It was five years before the first Atari and 13 years before the first Nintendo; it had no sound or color and came with 28 games, including hockey, roulette, western shootout, and table tennis.

918) When the American Civil War started, Robert E. Lee didn't own any slaves, but Ulysses S. Grant did.

919) In Mozambique, human honey hunters work with wild birds known as honeyguides. The hunters use calls to bring out the honeyguides that find the hives in the cavities of baobabs and other tall trees. The humans break open the hives and remove the honey and leave behind the wax and larvae for the honeyguides, one of the few birds who can digest wax.

920) Sharks existed 200 million years before the dinosaurs and have changed relatively little.

921) The number zero with its own unique value and properties did not exist until the 7th century in India. Before that, early counting systems only saw zero as a placeholder, not a true number.

922) By slowing their heart rate, sloths can hold their breath for 40 minutes.

923) In protecting their hives from outsiders, bees will sometimes sting other bees.

924) Koala bear fingerprints are virtually indistinguishable from human fingerprints, even with careful analysis under a microscope. They have the same loopy, whirling ridges as humans.

925) Sleep seems to clean the brain of harmful toxins. During sleep, the flow of cerebrospinal fluid in the brain increases dramatically, washing away harmful waste proteins that build up in the brain during waking hours.

926) In Switzerland, it is illegal to own just one guinea pig because they are social animals, and it is considered animal cruelty to deny them companionship.

927) On a per weight basis, spider silk has a tensile strength five times greater than steel. Each strand is 1,000 times thinner than a human hair and is made up of thousands of nanostrands, only 20 millionths of a millimeter in diameter.

928) The earth's continental plates drift about as fast as human fingernails grow.

929) To absorb urine and feces, both male and female astronauts wear a maximum absorbency garment, an adult diaper with extra absorption material, during liftoff, landing, and extra-vehicular activity. These operations can take a long time or have significant delays, and astronauts can't just get up and go to the bathroom at any time.

930) Different cells in the human body have very different lifespans. Sperm cells have a lifespan of about 3 days; colon cells die after about 4 days; white blood cells live for about 13 days. Cells in the top layer of your skin live about 30 days; red blood cells live for about 120 days; liver cells live about 18 months, and brain cells typically last an entire lifetime.

931) The footprints left behind by astronauts on the moon could last 10 to 100 million years. The moon has no atmosphere, so there is no wind or water to blow or wash anything away.

932) In space due to the lack of gravity, the mucus that normally empties through your nose and drains down the throat backs up in the sinuses. The only way to get rid of it is to blow your nose.

933) Charles Darwin ate many of the animal species he discovered.

934) In a study, the smell of Crayola crayons was among the top 20 most frequently identified smells. The unique smell is largely due to stearic acid, a derivative of beef fat used to create the waxy consistency.

935) In 1964, Donal Rusk Currey, a grad student, got his tree corer stuck in a bristlecone pine, and a park ranger helped him remove the tool, by cutting the tree down. When Currey counted the rings, he found out the tree was almost 5,000 years old, the oldest ever recorded at that time.

936) The lunula is the white crescent near the base of your fingernail.

937) Ancient Rome had 24 hours in a day, but their hours varied in length based on the time of year. They ensured that there were 12 hours of daylight and 12 hours of darkness, adjusting the length of the hours accordingly.

938) At its triple point, a liquid can exist simultaneously as a liquid, solid, and gas. The triple point is the temperature and pressure that puts the three states of matter into a thermodynamic equilibrium, where no state is trying to change into any other state. The boiling liquid causes high energy molecules to rise as a gas, which lowers the temperature of the boiling liquid and makes it freeze. The cycle continues if the triple point temperature and pressure are maintained. For water, the triple point is at 32.02 degrees Fahrenheit and 0.006 atmospheres (normal pressure is 1 atmosphere).

939) In early Greece and Rome, it was essentially impossible to understand a text on a first reading. There was no punctuation or spacing and no distinction between uppercase and lowercase letters; text was just a run-on string of letters.

940) The highest fall that a person ever survived without a parachute is 33,330 feet due to an airplane explosion in 1972. The survivor spent several days in a coma and many months in the hospital but made an almost complete recovery.

941) One of the largest living things in the world is Pando, a clonal colony of quaking aspen. It occupies 106 acres and weighs an estimated 6,600 tons in total. It has a single massive root system, estimated to be 80,000 years old. A clonal colony is a group of genetically identical individuals that have grown from a single ancestor. Pando is in the Fishlake National Forest in Utah.

942) Since 1994, all dogs are banned from Antarctica because they might introduce diseases that could transfer to the native seals.

943) The original constitution of the United States included an open invitation for Canada to join the United States. Ratified in 1781, the Articles of Confederation were replaced by the U.S. Constitution in 1789. If Canada agreed to become a member of the United States, there was a clause stating they would automatically be accepted without the consent of the other states.

944) Fish yawn, cough, and burp.

945) Mosquitos are by far the deadliest animal in the world, killing over 700,000 people annually worldwide primarily from malaria. Snakes are the second-most deadly animal, killing about 50,000 people; dogs are third, killing about 25,000 people mainly through rabies. Crocodiles are the deadliest of the large animals, killing about 1,000 people worldwide. The hippopotamus is the world's deadliest large land mammal, killing an estimated 500 people per year.

946) Researchers locate penguin colonies by looking for the stain trail from their droppings via satellite. It is easier to see than looking for the penguins themselves.

947) The cougar has more names than any other animal, such as puma, mountain lion, panther, catamount, or one of another 40 English, 18 native South American, and 25 native North American names.

948) In the last century, the east coast of the United States has moved about eight feet further away from Europe.

949) Pencils are typically yellow because it is the traditional color of Chinese royalty. In the 1890s when pencils started to be mass-produced, the best graphite came from China, and manufacturers wanted people to know they used the best quality graphite, so they painted them yellow, the color of Chinese royalty.

950) The youngest signer of the United States Declaration of Independence was Edward Rutledge, a lawyer from South Carolina who was only 26 at the time. Benjamin Franklin was the oldest signer at 70.

951) Without saliva, you wouldn't be able to taste your food. Enzymes in your saliva break down the food and release molecules that are picked up by your taste buds.

952) The sound you hear when you hold a seashell to your ear is surrounding environmental noise resonating in the seashell cavity. In a soundproof room, you don't hear anything when you hold a seashell to your ear.

953) The difference between antlers (found on deer, elk, and moose) and horns (found on pronghorn antelope, bighorn sheep, and bison) is that antlers are an extension of the animal's skull, and they are true bone that is shed and regrown each year. Horns are composed of an interior bone that is an extension of the skull; they are covered by an exterior sheath, grown by specialized hair follicles. They aren't shed and continue to grow throughout the animal's life. The exception is the pronghorn antelope, which sheds and regrows its horn sheath each year.

954) The liver is the only human internal organ that can regenerate itself. You can lose up to 75% of your liver, and the remaining portion can regenerate into a whole liver. Therefore, living donor liver transplants can be done, where a portion of the liver is taken, and both the donor and recipient's portion regrows into a full liver within about four months. A liver from a deceased donor may also be split and transplanted into two recipients.

955) The technical term for a cat's hairball is bezoar. The term also applies to a mass of indigestible material found in the gastrointestinal tract of other animals, including humans.

956) To cure a toothache in ancient Egypt, people put a dead mouse cut in half in their mouth.

957) Red is the rarest human hair color, with less than 2% of the world's population.

958) About 20% of the world's households don't have a television.

959) A fire rainbow looks like a rainbow in the clouds, but it is technically called a circumhorizontal arc. It occurs when the sun is higher than 58° above the horizon and its light passes through high-altitude cirrus clouds made up of hexagonal plate ice crystals. When aligned properly, the ice crystals act as a prism, resulting in refraction that looks like a rainbow in the clouds.

960) The word "computer" is referenced as far back as the early 1600s, but it originally meant a person who did arithmetic calculations. It didn't take on its meaning of being a machine until the late 1800s and an electronic device until the mid-1900s.

961) Although the triggering mechanism is different, dead people can get goosebumps. As rigor mortis sets in, muscles contract, and the arrector pili muscles, attached to the hair follicles, also contract to produce goosebumps.

962) You can get from Norway to North Korea by land going through just one country, Russia.

963) The letter j was the last letter added to the English alphabet. The letters i and j were treated the same for a long time until Italian Gian Giorgio Trissino made the distinction between them in 1525; j finally entered the alphabet in the 19th century.

964) The word "robot" was first used in a 1920 play called *Rossum's Universal Robots*. It comes from the Slavic word "rabota," meaning slave labor.

965) In case their pants split, major league baseball umpires are required to wear black underwear.

966) Chameleons don't change their colors for camouflage purposes. They change color by stretching and relaxing cells that contain crystals, which affects how the light is reflected, but their primary purposes for changing color are to communicate with other

chameleons (dark colors signal aggression) and to regulate their temperature (lighter colors reflect the heat).

967) Paper cuts hurt more than other cuts for a combination of reasons. They most often occur on the tips of the fingers that have more pain receptors than almost anywhere else in the body, and paper edges also aren't as smooth as they appear and can leave a rough cut. Finally, paper cuts aren't deep enough to trigger some of the body's defense mechanisms, like blood clotting and scabbing, so the damaged nerve endings remain exposed.

968) When you shuffle a deck of 52 cards, there are so many possible sequences that it is statistically likely that a well-shuffled deck is in a sequence that has never occurred before and will never occur again. There are $8.07 \times 10^{67}$ possible sequences for a deck of 52 cards; there are only about $10^{24}$ stars in the observable universe.

969) Female cats are significantly more likely to be right paw dominant, and male cats typically favor their left paw. Cats don't seem to have an overall preference for right or left, and researchers theorize their preferences are linked to neural differences.

970) Mushrooms are more closely related to humans than they are to plants. Animals and fungi branched off from plants about 1.1 billion years ago; later, animals and fungi separated genealogically, making mushrooms closer to humans than to plants.

971) The longest recorded time a chicken has flown continuously is 13 seconds. The longest distance chicken flight ever recorded is 301.5 feet.

972) The earth's surface curves out of sight at about 3.1 miles.

973) Venus rotates so slowly that you could watch a sunset forever by walking towards it. At the equator, Venus rotates 4 mph; the Earth rotates 1,038 mph at the equator.

974) When the queen of a bee colony becomes too old or unproductive, the worker bees dispose of her by clustering around her in a tight ball until she overheats and dies. The process is known as "cuddle death" or "balling."

975) There are multiple times more deaths caused by taking selfies each year than there are by shark attacks.

976) Abstemious and facetious are the only two words in the English language that have all five vowels in order.

977) The average human body worldwide has a volume of about 2.22 cubic feet.

978) The giant clam is the largest mollusk and can reach 4 feet in length and weigh more than 500 pounds. They live in the warm waters of the South Pacific and Indian Oceans and can live more than 100 years.

979) Platypuses sweat milk. Like other mammals, they secrete milk from mammary glands, but they don't have nipples, so the milk oozes from the surface of their skin, more like sweat. Because the delivery system is less hygienic, platypus milk contains antibacterial proteins to protect the babies.

980) Horseshoe crabs have 10 eyes, spread all over their body; they have eyes on top of their shell, on their tail, and near their mouth.

981) On the day he was shot at Ford's Theatre, Abraham Lincoln signed legislation creating the U.S. Secret Service. The original mission of the Secret Service was solely to combat currency counterfeiting; it wasn't until 1901, after the killing of two more presidents, that it was also tasked with protecting the president.

982) A googleganger is a person with the same name who shows up in results when you Google yourself.

983) Crayola means oily chalk. It combines the French word "craie," meaning chalk, with "ola," shortened from the French word "oléagineux," meaning oily.

984) If they are swimming near each other, alligators will always give manatees the right of way.

985) At its peak, the British Empire was the largest empire by area in history; in 1922, it ruled over about 24% of the world's land.

986) In the human body, there are about 200 different kinds of cells, and within those cells, there are about 20 different kinds of structures.

987) When Disneyland opened in 1955, Tomorrowland was designed to look like 1986, the distant future.

988) When you read to yourself, your tongue and vocal cords still get movement signals from the brain. The process is known as subvocal speech and is characterized by minuscule movements in the larynx and other muscles involved in the articulation of speech; the movements are undetectable without the aid of machines.

989) Technically, United States Independence Day is July 2, 1776, which is when Congress voted America free from British rule. July 4 is the day the Declaration of Independence was adopted.

990) Crapulous is the feeling you get from eating or drinking too much.

991) The medical name for the human butt crack is the intergluteal cleft.

992) King Sobhuza II of Swaziland ruled for 82 years and 254 days, the longest verifiable reign of any monarch in recorded history. Sobhuza reigned from 1899 until 1982.

993) To become butterflies, caterpillars essentially dissolve themselves. In the cocoon, the caterpillar releases enzymes that dissolve all its tissues. It then begins rapid cell division to form an adult butterfly or moth.

994) Ravens, crows, jays, and some songbirds lie in anthills and roll around, letting the ants swarm on them, or they chew up the ants and rub them on their feathers. It is called anting, and it isn't understood why they do it.

995) Mapmakers have a long tradition of putting slight inaccuracies in their maps to catch people who may try to copy their work. Typically, it is something small like a nonexistent dead-end, fake river bend, or adjusted mountain elevation. However, in one case, a mapmaker put in the fictional town of Agloe, New York. When a store was built in the corresponding location, the owner read the map and named it Agloe General Store, assuming that was a real area name, so a fictional location became real.

996) At the Palace of Versailles, there were no restrooms, so people would just defecate in the corners. Visitors often complained about how bad the palace smelled, and King Louis XIV ordered that the hallways be cleaned of feces at least once a week, and they brought in potted orange trees to mask the smell.

997) On average, a person grows 450 miles of hair on their head over their lifetime.

998) The Amazon rainforest produces more than 20% of the world's oxygen.

999) During a typical lifetime, people spend about six years dreaming.

1000) *The Simpsons* has been the longest-running primetime scripted show on U.S. television longer than any other show in history; it has been the longest-running show since July 1998.

1001) The force required to topple a domino is less than the force it generates when it falls; this force amplification can be used to topple ever-larger dominos. Each domino can be about 1.5 times larger than the preceding one. Starting with a regular size domino at about 1.875

inches tall, the 25th domino toppled would be about 2,630 feet tall, about the height of the tallest building in the world.

1002) Your right ear is better at receiving sounds from speech, and your left ear is more sensitive to sounds of music.

1003) At 4,300 miles long, the Andes are the longest above-water mountain range in the world, but the mid-ocean ridge, at 25,097 miles, is the longest if you include underwater ranges. The mid-ocean ridges of all the world's oceans are connected.

1004) Lobsters have urine release nozzles right under their eyes, and they urinate as a way of communicating with each other.

1005) Dogs normally start sniffing with their right nostril and keep using the right nostril if the smell is something unpleasant or potentially dangerous. If the smell is something pleasant, they will switch to use their left nostril.

1006) By mass, the Etruscan shrew is the smallest mammal, weighing about 0.06 ounces on average. The shrew has a very fast metabolism and eats 1.5 to 2 times its body weight per day. It also has the fastest heartbeat of any mammal, 1,500 beats per minute.

1007) Male pandas perform a handstand when they urinate. By doing the handstand, they get their pee higher up the tree, allowing their scent to be carried further and increasing their mating chances.

1008) Reindeer eyes change color from gold in summer to blue in winter. During bright summer light, their eyes reflect most light and look gold; during winter, the tissue behind their retina becomes less reflective, and their eyes appear blue. This increases their light sensitivity and vision in the low winter light.

1009) All the gold ever mined in the history of the world would fit in a 67-foot cube.

1010) The world's largest recorded turtle was a leatherback turtle that washed up on Harlech Beach, Wales, in 1988. It was estimated to be 100 years old and was almost 9 feet long and weighed 2,016 pounds.

1011) Even though Froot Loops cereal has a variety of colors, all colors have the same flavor, a fruit blend.

1012) Over the last 20,000 years, the size of the average human brain has shrunk by about 10%. There are no clear answers to why.

1013) Due to spinal decompression, you are about one centimeter taller when you wake up in the morning.

1014) Dysania is the state of finding it hard to get out of bed in the morning.

1015) $1.19 (three quarters, four dimes, and four pennies) is the most money you can have in change and not be able to make change for a dollar.

1016) Despite what you see in the movies, Roman warships were not rowed by slaves. Only free Roman citizens had a duty to fight for the state; in exceptional times if they needed more men, they would admit slaves to the military, but they were either freed before enlisting or promised freedom if they fought well.

1017) An autological word is a word that describes itself; some examples include noun, word, polysyllabic, unhyphenated, and suffixed.

1018) Ravens can learn to talk better than some parrots, and they also mimic other noises, including other animals and birds. They have even been known to imitate wolves or foxes to attract them to a carcass to break it open, so the raven can get at it when they are done.

1019) A male dog lifts his leg to pee because he wants to leave his mark as high as possible, as a sign of size and status. He also prefers to pee on vertical objects because the scent lasts longer.

1020) Pepperoni was created in America in the early 20th century.

1021) Ironically, dentists helped popularize cotton candy. In 1897, machine-spun cotton candy was invented by John C. Wharton, a candy maker, and William Morrison, a dentist. They called it fairy floss and sold thousands of servings at the 1904 St. Louis World's Fair. In 1921, Joseph Lascaux, a dentist, patented another machine and was the first to use the name cotton candy.

1022) The farthest object visible to the naked human eye is the Andromeda Galaxy, 2.6 million light-years away. It is visible as a dim, large, gray cloud almost directly overhead in a clear night sky.

1023) Toilet paper traces its origins to at least 6th century China when it was first referenced in writings. Most people didn't use toilet paper until at least 1857 when American inventor Joseph Gayetty commercialized the product much as we know it today.

1024) The small bump on the inner corner of your eye is the caruncula.

1025) Urohidrosis is the habit of some birds of defecating onto their legs and feet to cool themselves. For birds, solid and liquid wastes are expelled together, so it is a liquid mixture of feces and urine.

Flamingos, several species of storks, and some vultures exhibit this behavior.

1026) The state name Idaho was proposed by a lobbyist, who claimed it was a Shoshone word meaning "Gem of the Mountains"; in reality, he just made it up.

1027) In *Star Wars Episode V: The Empire Strikes Back*, Darth Vader never says, "Luke, I am your father." Instead, he says, "No, I am your father."

1028) You can't hum while holding your nose; to create the humming sound, air must escape through your nose.

1029) Its purpose isn't known, but about 39% of the population has a bone in their knee called the fabella. From historical studies, the percentage fell from 17% in 1875 to 11% in 1918, before rising to the current number.

1030) In the 18th and 19th centuries, squirrels were popular pets. They were sold in pet shops and were a preferred pet among the wealthy.

1031) While he was in office, President Ulysses S. Grant was arrested and taken into custody for speeding with a horse and buggy in Washington, D.C. The police seized his horse and buggy, and he paid a fine and walked back to the White House.

1032) Early humans in South America hunted giant armadillos that were about the size and weight of a Volkswagen Beetle; they used their shells for homes.

1033) The Pilgrims didn't first land at Plymouth Rock; they first landed in what is now Provincetown, Massachusetts, and signed the Mayflower Compact there. They arrived at Plymouth Rock five weeks later.

1034) Only 5% of the universe is made up of normal matter; 25% is composed of dark matter; 70% is dark energy.

1035) The state of Virginia extends further west than West Virginia.

1036) Junk email is called spam because of Monty Python. The 1970 *Monty Python's Flying Circus* sketch where a waitress reads a menu with an endless variety of Spam options and a chorus of Vikings sings "Spam, Spam, Spam, Spam" resulted in spam being used generically for something that drowns out or overrides everything else, as junk email does.

1037) In the 15th century, King Louis XI of France ordered Abbot de Beigne to create a musical instrument using the voices of pigs. He built a keyboard that jabbed a spike into the rumps of pigs to produce a squeal.

1038) Uranus was originally called Planet George, in honor of English King George III.

1039) If you wanted to dig a hole straight through the center of the earth and end up in China, you would have to start in Argentina.

1040) With two exceptions, China owns all the giant pandas in the world. Any panda in a foreign zoo is on loan from China, with the agreement that China owns the panda and any offspring which must be returned to China before they are four years old. The only exceptions are two pandas China gave to Mexico before implementing the current policy.

1041) Every second, the sun produces as much energy as over 90 billion one-megaton nuclear bombs.

1042) Depending on the type of impulse, nerve signals in the human body travel at different speeds. Muscle position impulses travel at speeds up to 266 mph; pain signals travel much slower, only 1.4 mph, and touch signals travel at 170 mph. You feel the touch that produces the pain 2-3 seconds before you feel the associated pain.

1043) McDonald's uses over 10% of the potatoes harvested in the United States annually.

1044) Melanistic animals are the opposite of albinos. They are all black, instead of all white, and have an excess of melanin that makes their skin, hair, or fur very dark or black.

1045) The sign we know as the ampersand (&) was the 27th letter of the English alphabet before being dropped. It wasn't called an ampersand at that time and was referred to as "and."

1046) A group of hippos is called a bloat.

1047) Zambia has a larger percent of its area devoted to national parks than any other country; national parks make up 32% of its area.

1048) Sound travels over four times faster in water than it does in air.

1049) The Great Pyramid of Giza was originally covered in highly polished white limestone; it was removed over time, so it could be used for other building projects.

1050) It is illegal to take pictures of the Eiffel Tower at night. French copyright law gives the original creator of an object exclusive rights to its sale and distribution; this includes buildings and lasts for 70 years after death. Gustave Eiffel, the tower creator, died in 1923, which means the copyright ran out in 1993 making the likeness and design public domain at that point. The Las Vegas replica wasn't built until 1999. Night photos are still protected by copyright; the Eiffel Tower lights were installed in 1985 and are considered a separate artistic work by their creator, Pierre Bideau, and protected by copyright until 70 years after his death.

1051) In 1958, a B-47 carrying an atomic bomb, larger than the one dropped on Nagasaki, accidentally dropped it on Mars Bluff, South Carolina. The core of the bomb was still on the plane, so there wasn't a nuclear explosion, but the 6,000 pounds of conventional high explosives detonated. The bomb fell on a garden in a rural area and created a 35-foot-deep by 75-foot-wide crater and destroyed the nearby house and outbuildings. Fortunately, no one was killed, and there were only minor injuries.

1052) In 1891 when electricity was first installed at the White House, President Benjamin Harrison and his wife were so afraid of being electrocuted that they never touched the light switches; they always had staff turn the lights on and off.

1053) Facebook has a blue color scheme because its founder, Mark Zuckerberg, has red-green color blindness, and blue is the color he sees best.

1054) During WWI, a Canadian soldier made a black bear his pet and named her Winnipeg. She was known as Winnie when she became a resident of the London Zoological Gardens, where a boy named Christopher Robin, son of author A.A. Milne, adored her and named his teddy bear after her.

1055) The average Major League Baseball game lasts almost 3 hours, but it only has about 18 minutes of action if you include balls in play, stolen base attempts, pitches, running batters, pickoff throws, etc. If you just include balls in play and runner advancement attempts, there are less than 6 minutes of action.

1056) Time passes faster for your face than it does for your feet. The difference is much too small for humans to perceive, but technically, time passes faster at higher elevations because the pull of the earth's gravitational field is weaker. Researchers have proven the differences, even with height differences less than one meter.

1057) Pluto hadn't even made one complete revolution around the sun between its discovery as a planet and its demotion to dwarf planet. Pluto was discovered in 1930, and it takes 248 years for it to complete one rotation around the sun, so its first birthday (one Pluto year) since discovery won't be until 2178.

1058) In 1838, Edgar Allan Poe published the novel *The Narrative of Arthur Gordon Pym of Nantucket* that describes how the crew of a ship, the *Grampus*, were adrift in the ocean and drew straws to decide who would be eaten. The losing crew member was Richard Parker, who was killed and eaten. Forty-six years later in 1884, a yacht, the *Mignonette*, sank, and its four surviving crew escaped in a lifeboat. They eventually decided they were going to have to eat one of their own to survive. They killed and ate a crew member named Richard Parker.

1059) Atoms are 99.9999999% empty space. If all the empty space was eliminated, the entire human species would fit into the volume of a sugar cube.

1060) In 2009, physicist Stephen Hawking threw a champagne party for time travelers. He didn't put out invitations until after the party; if someone showed up, he hypothesized that it would be proof of time travel. No one came.

1061) President Martin Van Buren helped to make the word "ok" popular. Based on the town he was from in New York, one of his nicknames was "Old Kinderhook"; during his presidential campaign, people held up signs and chanted "OK."

1062) Chocolate has been used as medicine since at least the 1500s. The Aztecs brewed a drink from cacao and tree bark to treat infections. Children with diarrhea received a drink made from the grounds of cacao beans and other roots. A text from 1552 lists a host of ailments cacao could treat including angina, fatigue, dysentery, gout, hemorrhoids, and even dental problems.

1063) Hippos sleep in the water; they surface automatically and breathe without waking up.

1064) On average, female anaconda snakes are 4.7 times larger than males; that is the largest size difference between sexes in any land vertebrate.

1065) Reindeer can see ultraviolet light. The human eye blocks UV light from reaching the retina, and in situations with a lot of reflected UV light, like snow, it can damage the eye, causing snow blindness. For reindeer, who must deal with reflected UV light from arctic snow most of the year, it makes sense they would develop a way of seeing into the UV light to protect themselves from snow blindness, but it also helps them in their survival. Important things like urine from predators or competitors, fur from predators, and lichen, one of their main food sources in the winter, absorb UV light and appear black against the snow, making them easy to see.

1066) Sloths only poop once a week; they also must do it on the ground, making them an easy target for predators. A sloth can lose one-third of its body weight from pooping, and it all comes out in one push. They dig a small hole to go in and cover it up when they are done and head back into the trees.

1067) Sometime between 1268 and 1300, the first pair of corrective eyeglasses were invented in Italy; they were two reading stones (magnifying glasses) connected with a hinge. They were balanced on the bridge of the nose.

1068) Cockroaches have existed for about 350 million years; they were around 120 million years before dinosaurs.

1069) A mondegreen is a mishearing or misinterpretation of a phrase in a way that gives it a new meaning, such as when you mishear the lyrics of a song and insert words that sound similar and make sense.

1070) Seahorses don't have teeth or stomachs and must eat constantly, so they don't starve.

1071) When you blush, your stomach lining also turns red due to increased blood flow throughout the body from the release of adrenaline.

1072) Memories continually change. They are malleable and are reconstructed with each recall; what we remember changes each time we recall the event. The slightly changed memory becomes the current memory, only to be reconstructed with the next recall.

1073) At any given time, there are about 1,800 thunderstorms in progress around the world. About 18 million thunderstorms occur annually worldwide; the United States has 100,000 to 125,000 thunderstorms annually.

1074) In 2014 when Queen Elizabeth II visited the *Game of Thrones* set in Belfast, Northern Ireland, she declined an opportunity to sit on the Iron Throne because there is an old tradition that prohibits the reigning English monarch from even sitting on a foreign throne.

1075) Giraffes can't cough because their lungs are too far away from their epiglottis, and coughing is a combination movement of the lungs and epiglottis.

1076) FDA regulations allow a certain amount of foreign animal matter to be present in food. For raisins, 10 insects and 35 fruit fly eggs per 8 ounces are acceptable; for peanut butter, 5 rodent hairs and 150 bug fragments in 1 pound is fine.

1077) Scientists believe that it rains diamonds on Jupiter and Saturn. Lightning storms turn methane into soot that under pressure hardens into chunks of graphite and then diamond as it falls. The largest diamonds would likely be about a centimeter in diameter and would eventually melt in the hot planet core.

1078) The slow loris is the only known venomous primate. They are nocturnal and live in southeast Asia. If they lick a gland under their arms and combine it with their saliva, they have a toxic bite.

1079) Everyone who has walked on the moon was born before 1936. Charles Duke, the tenth person to walk on the moon, was born the latest, October 3, 1935.

1080) The surface area of your lungs is about the same size as a tennis court.

1081) When written out in English, no number before one thousand contains the letter a.

1082) Ester Ledecka, of the Czech Republic, is the first woman to win gold medals in two different sports at the same Winter Olympics. At the 2018 PyeongChang Olympics, she won in skiing and snowboarding.

1083) Before 1824, no one knew that dinosaurs had existed. Even though the name dinosaur wasn't applied until 1842, William Buckland, a geology professor at Oxford, was the first person to recognize dinosaurs when he used the name Megalosaurus to describe an extinct carnivorous lizard fossil.

1084) A photon of light takes about 8 minutes to get from the sun to the earth, but it can take a photon 100,000 years to get from the core of the sun to the surface.

1085) The 3 Musketeers candy bar got its name because it originally came in a package that had three pieces with different nougat flavors: vanilla, chocolate, and strawberry.

1086) Until about 10,000 years ago, all humans had brown eyes. A genetic mutation at about that time produced blue eyes.

1087) Niddick is the term for the nape of the neck.

1088) Lyme disease gets its name from Lyme, Connecticut, a small coastal town where several cases were identified in 1975.

1089) President John Quincy Adams received a pet alligator as a gift and kept it in the White House East Room bathroom for two months before returning it.

1090) Compared to humans, cats have six to eight times more rod cells in their eyes; the rods are sensitive to low light, giving them their superior night vision. Their elliptical eye shape and larger corneas also help gather more light.

1091) About 100 cats roam free at Disneyland; they keep the rodent population down and have been in the park since it opened in 1955. They're all spayed, neutered, vaccinated, and tagged and have feeding stations, veterinary care, and are taken care of by the workers.

1092) With one ship and seven men, Mongolia has the smallest navy in the world; it is the world's second-largest landlocked country.

1093) When Thomas Jefferson sent Lewis and Clark on their expedition, he asked them to look for wooly mammoths; Jefferson believed that there might be wooly mammoths still living in the west.

1094) The first U.S. car race ever was on Thanksgiving Day, November 27, 1895. The *Chicago-Times Herald* sponsored a 54-mile race from downtown Chicago to Evanston and back. The top speed of the winning car was 7 mph.

1095) Scientists have tracked Alpine swifts, a swallow-like bird found in Europe, Africa, and Asia, that can fly for 200 days straight. They eat and sleep while flying and never leave the air.

1096) Wisconsin is known as the Badger State because lead miners in the 1830s lived in temporary caves cut into the hillsides that became known as badger dens, and the miners who lived in them were known as badgers.

1097) Due to the U.S. Electoral College, you would only theoretically need 23% of the popular vote to win the presidential election. This requires winning the required 270 electoral votes in the smallest electoral vote states by one vote in each state and not getting any votes in the largest electoral vote states.

1098) Whales, dolphins, orcas, and porpoises have an unusual form of sleep called unihemispheric slow-wave sleep. They shut down only one hemisphere of their brain and close the opposite eye. During this time, the other half of the brain monitors what is happening in their environment and controls breathing functions. Dolphins will sometimes hang motionless at the surface of the water during sleep, or they may swim slowly.

1099) South African earthworms are the largest known and can grow as long as 22 feet, with the average length being about 6 feet.

1100) Pocahontas was the first woman to appear on U.S. paper currency; in 1865, she appeared on the back of the $20 bill.

1101) Slave-maker ants will take over the nest of other ants, and when the new ants hatch, they become slaves of the colony.

1102) Humans make up about 0.01% of the earth's biomass; plants account for about 80%; bacteria account for 13%, and fungi are 2%. In total, animals account for about 0.36%, with insects making up about half of that and fish accounting for another third.

1103) A spider's muscles pull its legs inward, but they can't push them out again. To push them out, it must pump a watery liquid into its legs.

1104) The night Abraham Lincoln was assassinated he had a bodyguard, but he had left his post to have a drink at the Star Saloon, next to Ford's Theatre. John Frederick Parker was the police officer assigned to guard Lincoln and was initially seated outside the president's box. To be able to see the play, he moved to the first gallery, and at intermission, he joined the footman and coachman for Lincoln's carriage for drinks next door. It isn't clear if he returned to the theater at all, but he wasn't at his post outside Lincoln's box when John Wilkes Booth shot him. Ironically, Booth had been at the same saloon working up his courage. In November 1864, the Washington police force created the first permanent detail to protect the president; it was made up of four officers. The Secret Service did not begin protecting the president until 1901 after the assassination of President William McKinley.

1105) Based on his medical records, which were auctioned off in 2012, Adolf Hitler had a huge problem with flatulence. He was regularly taking 28 different drugs to try to control it. Some of the anti-gas pills he used contained a base of strychnine, which caused further stomach and liver issues.

1106) Cleopatra spoke as many as a dozen languages and was educated in mathematics, philosophy, oratory, and astronomy. She is often portrayed as being an incomparable beauty and little else, but there is also evidence that she wasn't as physically striking as once believed.

1107) Frogs can't swallow with their eyes open. Since they don't have muscles to chew their food, they use their eyes to force their food down their throats. Their eyes sink inside their skull, pushing the food down.

1108) To smell more attractive to females, male goats urinate on their heads.

1109) Some people who get bitten by the lone star tick can develop a sudden allergy to red meat. The allergy affects the sensitivity to a carbohydrate called galactose-alpha-1,3-galactose, which is in most mammal cell membranes, so the allergy doesn't extend to poultry or seafood. The lone star tick has been recorded as far north as Maine and as far west as central Texas and Oklahoma.

1110) As part of its reproductive process, the jewel wasp will sting a cockroach twice, first in the thorax to partially immobilize it and then in the head to block its normal escape reflex. The wasp is too small to carry the cockroach, so it leads it back to its burrow by pulling on one of its antennae. Once in the burrow, the wasp lays one egg on the roach's abdomen and exits and fills in the burrow entrance with pebbles. With the effect of the wasp venom, the roach rests in the burrow, and in about three days, the wasp's egg hatches, and the larva begins feeding on the roach for four to five days before chewing its way into the roach's abdomen. It continues to reside inside the roach, and over eight days, it consumes the roach's internal organs, in an order that maximizes the time the roach is still alive. The larva enters a pupal stage and forms a cocoon inside the roach, and the fully-grown wasp eventually emerges from the roach's body, completing the reproductive cycle.

1111) While there are more than 60 species of eagles worldwide, only two species, the bald eagle and the golden eagle, live in North America.

1112) The skin on a whale shark's back can be up to four inches thick, and they can make it even tougher by clenching the muscles just beneath the skin. Their underbellies are relatively soft and vulnerable, so they will often turn their belly away when approached.

1113) Opossums don't play dead; if frightened, they go into shock, which induces a comatose state that can last from 40 minutes to 4 hours.

1114) The words bulb, angel, and month have no rhyming words in the English language.

1115) Kinderschema is a set of physical characteristics that humans are naturally drawn towards; the characteristics include a rounded belly, big head, big eyes, loose limbs, etc. Puppies, kittens, and other animals, including human babies, trigger kinderschema. Humans have an intrinsic motivation to care for babies and children; these tendencies have developed through millions of years of evolution.

1116) Drupelets are the individual bumps making up a raspberry or blackberry.

1117) Typewriter is the longest English word that can be made using the letters on only one row of the keyboard.

1118) Hitler, Stalin, and Mussolini were all nominated for the Nobel Peace Prize.

1119) The time between the Stegosaurus and Tyrannosaurus Rex is larger than the time between the Tyrannosaurus and you. Stegosaurus existed about 150 million years ago; Tyrannosaurus Rex didn't evolve until about 67 million years ago, so the two were separated by about 83 million years.

1120) Australia has over 860 different reptile species, more than any other country in the world. They include lizards, crocodiles, turtles, and snakes. North America only has 280 reptile species.

1121) The human eye has enough visual acuity that you could see a candle flame 30 miles away on a dark night if the earth was flat.

1122) Due to continental drift, New York City moves one inch further away from London each year.

1123) At the 1912 Stockholm Olympics, a Japanese men's marathon runner had an official finishing time of 54 years, 8 months, 6 days, 5 hours, 32 minutes and 20.3 seconds. Shizo Kanakuri was an experienced runner and held the 25-mile world record when he went to the Stockholm games; he started the race, but temperatures of almost 90 degrees Fahrenheit forced him to drop out after more than 18 miles. He did not notify the officials, and feeling ashamed that he did not finish, he went quietly back to Japan and was listed as missing in the results. In 1967, a Swedish television show started looking for the missing marathon runner, and at the age of 75, Kanakuri was invited to Sweden for the 55th anniversary of the 1912 games. He was allowed to finish the race and receive an official time.

1124) Based on volume, all the humans in the world could fit in a cube 2,577 feet on each side, about 0.116 cubic miles.

1125) The saltwater crocodile is the world's largest reptile. They are up to 20 feet long and 3,000 pounds.

1126) Due to erosion, Niagara Falls has receded about seven miles over the last 12,500 years.

1127) The Walt Disney Company is the largest consumer of fireworks in the world and the second-largest purchaser of explosive devices, behind the U.S. Department of Defense.

1128) A semordnilap is a word that makes a completely different word spelled backward, such as stressed and desserts. The word semordnilap is palindromes spelled backward.

1129) There are so many possible iterations of a game of chess that no one has been able to calculate it accurately. In the 1950s, mathematician Claude Shannon came up with what is known as the Shannon Number that estimates the possible iterations between $10^{111}$ and $10^{123}$. In comparison, there are $10^{81}$ atoms in the known universe.

1130) If you don't swing your arms while walking, it requires about 12% more effort to walk, which is equivalent to walking about 20% faster.

1131) Hawaiian pizza is Canadian; it was invented in 1962 in Ontario, Canada.

1132) The nursery rhyme *Mary Had a Little Lamb* is based on the true story of Mary Sawyer of Sterling, Massachusetts, who as an 11-year-old was followed to school by her pet lamb. John Roulstone, a student a year or two older, handed Mary a piece of paper the next day with a poem he had written about it. In 1830, Sarah Josepha Hale, a well-known writer and editor, published *Poems for Our Children* that included a version of the poem.

1133) A pair of brown rats can produce 2,000 descendants in a year and up to 500 million descendants in three years.

1134) About 12% of people dream entirely in black and white. The exposure to color television seems to have had a significant impact on whether people dream in color; people who grew up with little access to color television dream in black and white about 25% of the time. In the 1940s before color television, the numbers were reversed, with about 75% of people reporting they dreamed in black and white.

1135) On a clear night in a dark area, you can see about 2,000 stars in the sky.

1136) Huh is the closest thing to a universal word. It means the same thing in every language, and everybody in almost every language says it.

1137) The magma chamber of hot and partly molten rock beneath Yellowstone National Park is large enough to fill the 1,000 cubic mile Grand Canyon 11 times over.

1138) Originating in Missouri, a series of earthquakes in 1811 and 1812 raised the soil beneath the Mississippi River and temporarily changed its course, causing it to flow backward.

1139) Roman charioteer Gaius Appuleius Diocles, who lived in the 2nd century, was one of the most celebrated ancient athletes and might be the best-paid athlete of all time. He raced four-horse chariots, and records show he won 1,462 out of the 4,257 races he competed in. He also seemed to be a showman, making many of his victories come from behind last-second victories which made him even more popular. He raced for 24 years and retired at age 42. His winnings amounted to the equivalent of 2,600 kg of gold, which considering the buying power at the time would make him a multi-billionaire in today's dollars.

1140) By area, 38% of the United States is further north than the most southern point of Canada. Middle Island in Lake Erie at 41.7 degrees north latitude is the southernmost point of land in Canada and is about the same latitude as Chicago.

1141) To allow greater flexibility running, a dog's shoulder blades are somewhat unattached to the rest of the skeleton. They have floating shoulders that aren't attached to any bones at the top but do have muscle and ligament attachments.

1142) Caterpillars have up to 4,000 muscles, including 248 muscles in their head alone; humans have about 650 muscles in total.

1143) President Thomas Jefferson wasn't fond of formal events, and he often greeted foreign dignitaries in his pajamas.

1144) The letter x likely became the symbol for a kiss because in the Middle Ages most people were illiterate and would sign documents with an x and then kiss it to show their sincerity.

1145) Wombats are the only animal in the world with cube-shaped poop. It appears to be due to the irregular shape and elasticity of their intestines.

1146) Barnacle geese chicks must jump off cliffs, sometimes hundreds of feet high, when they are as little as one day old and can't fly. Barnacle geese, which nest in the Arctic, protect their young from predators by nesting on high ledges and cliffs. They can't feed the babies in the nest, and the chicks must eat within 36 hours, so to get to the grass they need to eat, they must jump from their nest and hope to survive. Fortunately, the chicks are light and fluffy and usually survive the fall, even after bouncing off rocks.

1147) A group of Purdue engineering students made a licking machine, modeled after a human tongue, and found that it took an average of 364 licks to get to the center of a Tootsie Pop.

1148) A college football game registered as an earthquake. The Earthquake Game was played between LSU and Auburn on October 8, 1988, at LSU's Tiger Stadium, with a crowd of 79,431 spectators. Auburn led 6-0 with less than two minutes left when LSU drove down the field and eventually threw an 11-yard touchdown pass on fourth down. The crowd's reaction to the touchdown pass registered as an earthquake on a seismograph located about 1,000 feet from the stadium at LSU's Howe-Russell Geoscience Complex. A seismologist noticed the reading the next day.

1149) We don't know how many insect species exist; new beetles are discovered at a rate of one an hour. There are 350,000 named beetles, plus perhaps 8 million more unnamed.

1150) There is enough water in Lake Superior to cover all the land in North and South America in one foot of water.

1151) At up to 7 feet tall and 1,500 pounds, the moose is the largest species of deer.

1152) In Colombia and other South American countries, movie theaters sell spicy roasted ants that are munched the way American's enjoy popcorn.

1153) Uncoiled, a Slinky is 87 feet long.

1154) The whale shark is the largest current day shark; they can be up to 41 feet long and 47,000 pounds.

1155) When he first appeared in 1938, the original comics Superman couldn't fly; he could only jump the very specific distance of one-eighth of a mile. His flying ability first appeared in cartoons and radio plays; it wouldn't appear in comics until 1941.

1156) In a short spurt, a domestic cat can run up to 30 mph; the fastest speed a human has ever run is about 28 mph.

1157) The standard U.S. railroad width of 4 feet 8.5 inches is directly derived from the width of Roman war chariots. The English expatriates who designed the U.S. railroad system based their measurements on the pre-railroad tramways built in England, which were built using the same tools used to build wagons. To avoid breaking down during long treks across the old English roads created by the Romans, wagons were built to fit the ruts carved out by Roman war chariots, and all Roman chariots were built to a standard width of 4 feet 8.5 inches.

1158) Almost 3% of the ice in the Antarctic glaciers is from penguin urine.

1159) The little paper tail sticking out of a Hershey's Kiss is called a niggly wiggly.

1160) Giant anteaters eat up to 30,000 ants a day, and they sleep 16 hours a day.

1161) A baby owl is called an owlet.

1162) Cats and humans have almost identical brain structures, including the region which controls emotion. Cats have temporal, occipital, frontal, and parietal lobes in their brains, just like humans, and the connections within their brains seem to mirror those of humans. Their brains also release neurotransmitters, and they have short and long-term memory.

1163) Humans domesticated the horse around 4500 BC; the saddle was invented as early as 800 BC, but the stirrup probably wasn't created until about 300 BC.

1164) The Japanese Onagadori chicken has the world's longest feathers; its tail feathers can measure over 10 meters.

1165) In humans, the right lung is always larger than the left. The left lung is smaller to leave room for the heart.

1166) In 1879, Liege, Belgium, attempted to use 37 cats as mail carriers. Messages were placed in waterproof bags the cats carried around their necks. Not surprisingly, the cats proved to be unreliable and slow, taking many hours or a day to deliver the mail, and the service didn't last long.

1167) In ancient Egypt, if a patient died during surgery, the surgeon's hands were cut off.

1168) Without a visual reference point, humans are incapable of walking in a straight line. If blindfolded or lost in terrain devoid of landmarks, we tend to walk in circles. Scientists have yet been unable to determine why.

1169) Due to a global surge in jellyfish populations, nuclear power plants around the world are experiencing an increasing number of outages caused by jellyfish clogging cooling water intakes. Outages have occurred in Japan, Israel, Scotland, and the United States. The surging populations are likely due to overfishing reducing predation and the jellyfish's ability to withstand increasing ocean acidity levels.

1170) On average, it takes about a minute for human blood to circulate through the entire body.

1171) During WWI, starving wolves, displaced by the war, amassed in such numbers that the Germans and Russians agreed to a temporary cease-fire to jointly battle the wolves.

1172) In the 1920s when insulin was still harvested from animals, it took 10,000 pounds of pig pancreases to make 1 pound of concentrated insulin.

1173) Arachibutyrophobia is the fear of peanut butter sticking to the roof of your mouth.

1174) About 85% of humans only breathe out of one nostril at a time. They switch between nostrils about every four hours, although it varies by person, body position, and other factors.

1175) The Macy's Thanksgiving Day Parade used to intentionally release the giant inflatable balloon characters into the sky after the parade. The very first balloons would pop quickly, but in 1929, they added safety valves, so the helium would slowly leak out, allowing the balloons to float for days. They also tagged the balloons with return addresses, so they could be sent back to Macy's, who would reward the finders with gifts. When a balloon wrapped around an airplane's wing after the 1932 parade, they quit releasing the balloons; luckily, there were no fatalities.

1176) The first mutiny in space occurred on *Skylab 4* on December 28th, 1973. The three-man crew turned off radio communications with NASA for a full day and spent the day relaxing. They had already spent about as much time in space as anyone ever had and were tired of the demanding schedule NASA had set for them. After the day off, they continued their duties and spent about another month in space, setting the record at the time of 84 days.

1177) While a queen ant can live for up to 30 years, male ants typically only live for a few weeks, and workers live for several months.

1178) Adult dogs have 42 teeth; puppies have 28 baby teeth.

1179) The placebo effect works even if people know it is a placebo. If people were told the pill they were taking was a placebo but were also told that placebos can have an effect, they experienced the same outcome as those unknowingly taking a placebo.

1180) Ice worms are related to common earthworms, but they spend their entire lives in glaciers and require below freezing temperatures to survive. They are found across the northern United States and Canada and come to the surface of the glaciers to feed on snow algae. At temperatures even five degrees above freezing, their internal membranes start to fall apart, and they essentially liquefy and die.

1181) Thomas Jefferson kept a pair of grizzly bear cubs in a cage on the front lawn of the White House for a few months. They were a gift, and he decided they were too dangerous to keep and bequeathed them to a museum.

1182) Humans produce about 1.5 quarts of mucus per day and swallow most of it.

1183) Squirrels cause about 10-20% of all power outages in the United States. Squirrel outages tend to be more localized and more quickly fixed than those caused by storms.

1184) To produce one pound of honey, a hive of bees must visit 2 million flowers and fly about 55,000 miles. One bee colony can produce 60 to 100 pounds of honey per year. An average worker bee makes only about 1/12 of a teaspoon of honey in its lifetime and has a lifespan of about two months; queen bees typically live for three to five years.

1185) There is a chunk of Africa stuck under the United States. When the supercontinent Pangaea broke apart, about 250 million years ago, a chunk of Africa was left behind; it is located near Alabama, just off the coast.

1186) Snails move at a steady pace, with a maximum speed of about 50 yards per hour.

1187) Without its mucus lining, your stomach would digest itself. Stomach ulcers are areas where the stomach begins to digest itself.

1188) The longest English words with no repeating letters are two 15-letter words: uncopyrightable and dermatoglyphics.

1189) When poured, hot water has a higher pitch than cold water. Water changes viscosity with temperature, which affects the sound when poured.

1190) The vinculum is the line between two numbers in a fraction.

1191) The king rat can go longer without drinking than any other land animal; they can go their entire life, three to five years, without drinking.

1192) The surface area of Pluto is only about 3% larger than Russia.

1193) Parts of Canada have less gravity than they should. Since gravity is a result of mass, varying densities of the earth at different locations can affect it. However, the Hudson Bay region of Canada has a larger variation; the average resident weighs about a tenth of an ounce less than they would weigh elsewhere. The explanation appears to be the melting of the two-mile-thick Laurentide Ice Sheet that started melting about 21,000 years ago and is almost gone. The ice sheet left an indent in the earth, which means less mass and less gravity.

1194) On January 23, 1916, Browning, Montana, experienced the greatest temperature variation ever recorded in 24 hours. It had a 100-degree change, from a high of 44 degrees to a low of -56 degrees Fahrenheit.

1195) Owyhee is the original English spelling of Hawaii.

1196) About 1 in every 200 people is born with an extra rib; it is called a cervical rib and forms above the first rib, just above the collarbone. You can have a cervical rib on either or both sides, and it can be a fully-formed bony rib or a thin strand of tissue fibers.

1197) When a flea jumps, its acceleration is so intense that it must withstand 100 times the force of gravity. Humans pass out at about 5 times the force of gravity.

1198) Between 1853 and 1859, New York spent $7.4 million buying the 843 acres for Central Park; comparatively, the United States spent $7.2 million in 1867 to buy Alaska that is 663,268 square miles or 424 million acres.

1199) There is enough stone in the Great Pyramid of Giza to build a two-foot-tall by four-inch-wide wall around the entire earth.

1200) According to research, zebras likely evolved to have stripes to avoid biting flies. In an experiment, horses wearing a striped pattern coat had far fewer flies land on them than horses wearing a solid color coat. The flies spent the same amount of time circling, regardless of color, but far fewer landed with stripes.

# Facts 1201-1500

1201) Less than 1% of bacteria cause disease in humans.

1202) The human body is bioluminescent; it is just too faint for our eyes to see. A 2009 study found that human bioluminescence in visible light exists; the human body glimmers, but the intensity of the light emitted is 1,000 times lower than the sensitivity of our eyes.

1203) On average, a person will die from a complete lack of sleep faster than from starvation. You can live about 11 days without sleep but weeks without food.

1204) The average person has four to six dreams per night.

1205) The baobab tree can store up to 32,000 gallons of water in its trunk. Various species are native to Africa, Australia, and India; it can grow to almost 100 feet tall with a trunk diameter up to 36 feet and can live for thousands of years. Because it stores such large volumes of water in its trunk, elephants, eland, and other animals chew the bark during dry seasons.

1206) A double rainbow happens when light is reflected twice in the raindrop. You see two different reflections coming from different angles, and it also reverses the order of the colors on the secondary rainbow.

1207) Penguins can swim faster because they have a bubble boost, where they fluff their feathers and release bubbles that reduce the density of the water around them. The bubbles act as lubrication that decreases water viscosity.

1208) Human boogers are just dried mucus. Most mucus is swept by the nose cilia hair to the back of the throat, but some near your nostrils can begin to dry out first and become too thick to be swept by the cilia. If it sits long enough, it dries further and becomes a booger.

1209) Men account for about 90% of all shark attacks in the world. The reason is behavioral; men more frequently participate in the activities that put you at greatest risk for shark attacks, such as surfing, diving, and long-distance swimming. As women participate more in some of these risker activities, the number of female attacks is on the rise.

1210) Despite its western fame, the Pony Express was only in operation for 18 months, from April 1860 to October 1861. The route ran from St. Joseph, Missouri, to Sacramento, California, and could transport a letter over 1,800 miles in 10 days.

1211) In 1999 in North Carolina, a female skydiver's life was saved when her chutes didn't open and she landed on a mound of fire ants. She was jumping from 14,500 feet when her main parachute didn't open; her backup chute opened at 700 feet and quickly deflated. She hit the ground at about 80 mph, landing on a mound of fire ants that bit her over 200 times. Fire ants have a toxin-filled painful bite that can cause death in some cases. In this case, doctors determined that the repeated fire ant stings shocked her heart and stimulated her nerves and kept her heart beating and her organs functioning long enough to keep her alive during transport. She suffered shattered bones and was in a coma for two weeks, but she recovered fully.

1212) Wooly mammoths were still alive about 900 years after the Great Pyramid of Giza was built. The last mammoths died out about 1650 BC on Wrangel Island in the Arctic Ocean; the Great Pyramid was completed in about 2560 BC.

1213) Excluding eye injuries, pirates likely wore eye patches to see in the dark. They were constantly going above and below deck, and it takes the human eye up to 25 minutes to adapt to seeing in the dark. By wearing a patch, they kept one eye dark adjusted, so they could see in the dark immediately by moving the eye patch.

1214) Manatees control their buoyancy by farting. They can regulate the distribution of their intestinal gases, holding it in when they want to approach the surface and letting loose when it's time to sink.

1215) The only WWII U.S. mainland combat deaths occurred on May 5, 1945, when a Japanese balloon bomb exploded and killed a woman and five children in Oregon. The balloon bombs had a 33-foot diameter balloon with 35 pounds of explosives and were designed to rise to 30,000 feet and ride the jet stream east, making it from Japan to the United States in about three days. An altimeter would trigger a reaction that would jettison the bombs. Japan released about 9,000 of the bombs. A Sunday school teacher and five students happened upon an unexploded balloon bomb on the ground; it exploded while they were investigating it.

1216) Of the first five U.S. presidents, three died on July 4th. John Adams and Thomas Jefferson both died on July 4, 1826; James Monroe died five years later on July 4, 1831.

1217) The largest currency denomination ever printed in the United States is the 1934 $100,000 bill, featuring a picture of Woodrow Wilson. It was only printed for three weeks in December 1934 and January 1935, and they were only used for official transactions between Federal Reserve Banks.

1218) If you've ever yawned and had saliva shoot out your mouth, it is called gleeking. The salivary glands underneath your tongue become stimulated and shoot a concentrated jet of pure saliva; it typically happens when yawning.

1219) At up to 150 pounds, the South American capybara is the world's largest rodent.

1220) The use of the word "bucks" for dollars dates to the 1700s when deerskins were commonly used for trading. A trading record from 1748 notes the exchange of a cask of whiskey for 5 bucks. The term stayed around after the dollar became the U.S. standard currency in 1792.

1221) For centuries, families in central Europe have eaten carp for Christmas Eve dinner. In Slovakia and some nearby countries, the tradition goes further where the Christmas carp must first swim in the family bathtub for at least a day or two before being killed, cleaned, and prepared.

1222) Future president Theodore Roosevelt delivered an 84-minute campaign speech after being shot just before the event. He was shot as he stood up in an open-air automobile and waved his hat to the crowd; fortunately, the bullet was slowed by his dense overcoat, steel-reinforced eyeglass case, and 50-page speech squeezed into his jacket pocket. X-rays showed the bullet lodged against Roosevelt's fourth right rib on an upward path to his heart.

1223) Rats eat their feces for nutritional value.

1224) The word therein contains 10 words without rearranging any letters: the, there, he, in, rein, her, here, ere, therein, herein.

1225) The acnestis is the part of an animal's skin that it can't scratch itself, usually the area between the shoulder blades.

1226) In 1913, Adolf Hitler, Sigmund Freud, Marshal Tito, Leon Trotsky, and Joseph Stalin all lived in Vienna within walking distance of each other.

1227) The United Kingdom has more tornadoes per square mile than any other country.

1228) Theodore Roosevelt had a pet hyena named Bill, a present from the Emperor of Ethiopia.

1229) Thanks to the television series *MacGyver* that ran from 1985 until 1992 and was revived in 2016, the word MacGyver was added to the Oxford English Dictionary in 2015. As a verb, it means to make or repair an object in an improvised or inventive way, making use of whatever items are at hand.

1230) By area, Saudi Arabia is the largest country that doesn't have any natural rivers; it is the 12th largest country.

1231) North Korea has the highest percentage of its population in the military. Between active, reserves, and paramilitary, 30.8% of the entire population is in the military. Comparatively, 0.7% of the U.S. population is in the military.

1232) Rats don't sweat; they regulate their temperature by constricting or expanding blood vessels in their tails.

1233) Spraint is the dung of an otter.

1234) As a mosquito sucks your blood, they also pee on you. As they suck blood, mosquitoes need to get rid of excess fluid and salts, so they urinate to maintain their fluid and salt balance.

1235) A group of ravens is called an unkindness or conspiracy.

1236) Like other equines such as zebras and donkeys, horses have a single toe. Their ancient ancestors that lived 55 million years ago were dog-like in size and had 14 toes, four toes on their front feet and three on their back.

1237) According to recent studies, there may be about one trillion species of microbes, and 99.999% of them have yet to be discovered.

1238) Bulls don't see red. Cows, including bulls, are generally red-green colorblind; they are reacting to the motion of the fabric and not the color.

1239) As much as 95% of all dreams are forgotten shortly after waking. Research suggests that the changes in the brain during sleep do not support the information processing and storage for forming long-lasting memories.

1240) Virtually all barramundi fish are born male and turn into females after two years.

1241) Hippo milk is bright pink. Hippos secrete two unique acids, hipposudoric acid and norhipposudoric acid, that function as a natural sunscreen and antimicrobial agent. The acids are red and orange, and when mixed with a hippo mother's milk, they turn it bright pink.

1242) The termite queen is the longest living insect. They have been known to live for at least 50 years, and some scientists believe they may live to 100.

1243) Dogs tend to wag their tails more towards their right when they are relaxed and more to their left when they are afraid or insecure.

1244) Because of the severe damage caused by rabbits in Australia, it is illegal to own a pet rabbit for private purposes in Queensland, Australia. You can only have a rabbit for public entertainment or science and research.

1245) More than half the world's population lives within a 2,500-mile diameter circle in southeastern Asia. The circle incorporates 19 countries and 22 of the 37 cities in the world with 10 million or more population.

1246) About 1 in 8 American workers have worked at McDonald's at some point in their life.

1247) Thomas Jefferson did not like public speaking and preferred to remain quiet most of the time. He only made two speeches during his entire eight-year presidency; they were both inaugural speeches and were hardly audible.

1248) Male horses have more teeth than females. Males typically have 40 teeth; females have 36; the difference is that males usually have four canine teeth, located between the front incisors and the cheek teeth. Females don't usually have canine teeth.

1249) Early versions of the computer mouse were referred to as a turtle, rather than a mouse, presumably because of its hard shell on top.

1250) The Big Dipper isn't a constellation; it is an asterism. There are 88 official constellations in the night sky; any other grouping of stars that isn't one of the 88 is an asterism. In the Big Dipper's case, it is part of the Ursa Major (Great Bear constellation).

1251) It wasn't until the 1924 Indian Citizenship Act that Native Americans were granted full United States citizenship. The act was passed partially in recognition of the thousands of Native Americans that served in the military during WWI. The 14th amendment to the U.S. Constitution defines a citizen as any person born in the United States and subject to its jurisdiction, but the amendment had been interpreted to not apply to Native Americans.

1252) The first eight packs of Crayola crayons were sold door-to-door in 1903 for a nickel. Due to their poor paper adhesion, the creators felt they wouldn't appeal to artists, so they decided to market to children and educators.

1253) The black kite, whistling kite, and brown falcon are Australian birds of prey that intentionally spread fires. Aborigines have known this for centuries, and scientists have now confirmed it. These birds hang out around the edges of fires looking for escaping prey, and they will also pick up smoldering debris and fly up to a kilometer away and drop it to spread the fire. The act appears to be very intentional to create a new area where they can wait for prey escaping the fire.

1254) Because of the speed the sun moves, the maximum possible length for a solar eclipse is 7 minutes and 58 seconds.

1255) Research indicates that everyone dreams, whether they remember doing so or not.

1256) In humans, our two nostrils smell differently. Odors coming in through the right nostril are judged to be more pleasant, and you can describe odors coming in through your left nostril better. The difference is believed to be due to the right nostril being connected to the right brain, which deals more with emotions, and the left nostril is connected to the left brain, which deals more with language.

1257) Adult cats spend up to 50% of their waking time grooming.

1258) An ambigram is a word, art form, or other symbolic representation whose elements retain meaning when viewed or interpreted from a different direction, perspective, or orientation. For example, the word "swims" is the same when it is rotated 180 degrees.

1259) Dolphins call each other by name. Scientists have found evidence that dolphins use a unique whistle to identify each other.

1260) If you could fold an average thickness (0.004 inches) paper in half 42 times, it would be thick enough to reach the moon; if you could fold it 103 times, it would be 109 billion light-years thick, thicker than the observable universe is wide.

1261) The world record for a human going without sleep was set by 17-year-old Randy Gardner in 1964; he was intentionally awake for 11 days 25 minutes without any stimulants.

1262) There is no cellphone or Wi-Fi service in Green Bank, West Virginia because it could interfere with the operation of the National Radio Astronomy Observatory's radio telescope. The National Radio Quiet Zone was created in 1958 as an area where radio transmissions are heavily restricted by law. Straddling West Virginia's border with Virginia and Maryland, it covers a 13,000 square mile area. Restrictions apply to the entire area, but they are most severe the closer you get to the Green Bank Observatory.

1263) The philtrum is the groove in your upper lip that runs from the top of the lip to the nose.

1264) Walking takes about 200 muscles to take a single step.

1265) Gorillas are several times stronger than humans; a male silverback gorilla can lift 1,800 pounds.

1266) Velociraptors were nothing like they were portrayed in the movie *Jurassic Park*. They were about 3 feet tall and 6 feet overall (with tail); they had feathers and weighed about 30 pounds, the size of a large turkey.

1267) "In God We Trust" did not become the official U.S. national motto until 1956.

1268) The name M&M's stands for Mars & Murrie, the co-creators of the candy. Forest Mars, son of the Mars Company founder, and Bruce Murrie, son of the Hershey Chocolate president, went into business together in 1941 to develop the candy. Until 1949 when the partners had a falling out and Mars bought back Murrie's share of the business, M&M's contained Hershey's chocolate.

1269) American savant Kim Peek was the inspiration for the movie *Rain Man*; among his many abilities, he could read two pages of a book simultaneously. His left eye read the left page, and his right eye read the right page. Scans of his brain indicated that he didn't have the normal connections that transfer information between the left and right hemispheres, which may have been the reason for some of his abilities.

1270) The green sea slug, which lives off the east coast of the United States, is the first animal ever discovered that is also part plant. The slugs take chloroplasts into their skin, which turns them emerald green and makes them capable of photosynthesis. They can go without eating for nine months or more, photosynthesizing as they bask in the sun.

1271) If the salt in the oceans was removed and spread evenly over the earth's land surface, it would form a layer more than 500 feet thick.

1272) Antepenultimate means the third to last thing.

1273) Baby porcupines are called porcupettes.

1274) John F. Kennedy had a lifelong struggle with back pain and was wearing a tightly laced back brace that may have kept him from recoiling to the floor of his car after he was hit with the first bullet and made him an easier target for the second shot. The brace was a firmly bound corset around his hips and back; he tightly laced it and put a wide Ace bandage in a figure eight around his trunk, so his movement was significantly restricted.

1275) Australia's coastline is over 16,000 miles long, and it has over 10,000 beaches, more than any other country in the world.

1276) At the population density of New York City, the entire population of the world would fit in an area 9% larger than the state of Texas.

1277) Glass is neither a liquid nor a solid; it is an amorphous solid, a state somewhere between those two states of matter.

1278) Columella nasi is the fleshy end of your nose that splits your nostrils.

1279) When Colgate started mass producing its toothpaste in 1873, it was in a jar; they didn't put it in tubes until the 1890s.

1280) As is often the case, the Disney film *Pinocchio* was a much lighter take on the original story. The original does feature a talking cricket, although he isn't named Jiminy Cricket, but Pinocchio gets mad and kills the cricket after receiving some advice he doesn't like. Later, the talking cricket returns as a ghost to give Pinocchio additional advice.

1281) Dung beetles can navigate based on the position of the moon, sun, and stars. Researchers have found that they take a mental snapshot of the night sky and use it to find their way around. The beetles can recall their exact position, and when presented with an artificial sky, they change their course accordingly.

1282) The creature that most people identify as a daddy longlegs spider is not a spider at all; it is a long-legged harvestman, which is an arachnid but is not a spider. Harvestmen have one body section instead of the two spiders have, two eyes instead of eight, a segmented body instead of unsegmented, no silk, no venom, and a different respiratory system than spiders, among other differences.

1283) In August 1864, Abraham Lincoln was riding a horse to the Soldiers' Home outside of Washington, D.C., where the president and his family stayed to escape the summer heat. There was a gunshot, and his horse bolted; Lincoln lost his hat, which he believed was due to his horse jerking. When they went back to find his hat, they found a bullet hole in it; the assassination attempt was about eight months before John Wilkes Booth assassinated Lincoln.

1284) A domestic cat can't focus clearly on anything closer than about a foot away.

1285) When you peel a banana, the strings that come off are called phloem bundles; the strings distribute nutrients up and down the banana as it grows.

1286) With less than 400 residents, Ngerulmud, Palau, is the smallest population national capital in the world. Palau is an island nation in the Pacific Ocean.

1287) You never have been and never will be in the same physical location twice since the earth, our solar system, and our galaxy are all moving through space.

1288) Starfish don't have blood; their circulatory system is primarily made of seawater.

1289) About 70% of the atmospheric oxygen we breathe is produced by ocean plants, mainly by phytoplankton.

1290) 111,111,111 multiplied by 111,111,111 equals 12,345,678,987,654,321.

1291) During WWII in the Polish army, Private Wojtek carried ammunition to the frontline and was later promoted to corporal; he was a bear. He was also taught to salute.

1292) Compared to the Northern Hemisphere, toilet water in the Southern Hemisphere does not rotate in the opposite direction due to the Coriolis effect. The Coriolis force is a real effect and is why large systems, like hurricanes, do rotate in different directions in the two hemispheres, but it is proportional to velocity, and its effect on a toilet flushing is minuscule compared to the water jets and other irregularities.

1293) When touching and microwaved, two whole grapes or a pair of beads made mostly of water concentrate the energy from the microwaves at the point where they make contact and generate a very small hot spot intense enough to spark and generate plasma. The effect seems to be dependent on the size, composition, and shape of the objects.

1294) Christopher Columbus' three ships weren't likely called the Nina, Pinta, and Santa Maria. In the 15th century, most sailing ships were named after saints, so the Santa Maria is likely the real name, but the Nina and the Pinta were probably sailor nicknames. The Nina's real name was most likely the Santa Clara; the Pinta's real name is unknown.

1295) The primary reason dog noses are wet is because dogs secrete mucus that aids their sense of smell.

1296) Kangaroos continue to grow until they die.

1297) At an area of 43 square miles, Disney World is about the same size as the city of San Francisco.

1298) A gallon of gasoline contains about 31,000 calories; if you could drink gasoline as fuel, you could ride a bicycle at 15 mph for about 912 miles on a gallon of gas.

1299) The sound when you snap your finger is from the finger hitting the palm; it doesn't come from the finger rubbing the thumb.

1300) Some expensive perfumes still contain whale poop. Ambergris, a waxy substance produced in the intestines of sperm whales, has been incorporated in perfumes for a long time as a binding agent to help the fragrances linger on the skin and intensify the scent of the perfume. It has now been mostly replaced by synthetic alternatives.

1301) There are far more fake flamingos in the world than there are real ones. There are just under 2 million flamingos in the wild; there are many millions of plastic ones.

1302) At some points in history, money was designed to discourage people from having too much. According to Greek historian Plutarch, the Spartans used long, heavy iron rods as their currency to discourage people from pursuing great wealth. The currency was called obeloi and was so cumbersome that carrying multiple pieces would require help.

1303) Trees can tell if a deer is trying to eat them and defend themselves by producing astringent tannins that taste bad and put the deer off. When a bud is damaged, the tree can sense the animal's saliva in the wound, which triggers a hormone that causes it to increase the concentration of tannins in that part of the tree. It also spurs the tree to produce more growth hormones that cause the remaining buds to grow more vigorously and make up for those that have been lost to the deer.

1304) An adult blue whale's tongue weighs about 6,000–8,000 pounds, about the same as a small elephant.

1305) The earth receives more energy from the sun every hour than the entire world uses in a year. The earth receives about 430 quintillion joules of energy every hour from the sun, and we use about 410 quintillion joules of energy worldwide each year.

1306) About 98% of all the atoms in a human body are replaced every year.

1307) Sea otters have the densest fur of all animals; they have up to one million hairs per square inch on the densest parts of their bodies.

1308) When glass breaks, the cracks move at speeds up to 3,000 mph.

1309) A second is called a second because it was the second division of the hour; the original term was second minute.

1310) Despite being a ruthless warlord, Genghis Khan was very enlightened in his cultural and political policies as a ruler. He established freedom of religion, banned torture of prisoners, outlawed slavery, promoted people based on individual merit rather than birth, established universal law, created a writing system, instituted an international postal system, and redistributed the wealth he gained.

1311) Wendy's hamburgers are square because founder Dave Thomas took the phrase "not cutting corners" seriously, and he wanted the burgers to be square because the patties stick out of the bun in a way that showcases the meat's quality.

1312) Your fingers don't contain any muscles. The muscles that bend the finger joints are in the palm and mid-forearm and are connected to the finger bones by tendons that pull on and move the fingers.

1313) There are an estimated 10,000,000,000,000,000,000 (10 quintillion) insects alive at any given time.

1314) President Andrew Johnson was an indentured servant as a child. When he was three years old, his father passed away, and Johnson and his brother became indentured servants to a tailor; they worked for food and lodging. They both eventually ran away, and Johnson taught himself to read and worked as a tailor to support himself.

1315) Recent research has shown that the phrase "bloodcurdling" is physically accurate. The phrase can be traced back to medieval times when people believed that being scared could make your blood run cold or congeal. Studies have now shown that watching a horror film produces a significant increase in a blood-clotting protein. If you are frightened, the body seems to prepare itself for the possibility of blood loss.

1316) In 1799 in North Carolina, a 12-year-old boy found a 17-pound gold nugget in a creek and took it home; not realizing what it was, the family used it as a doorstop for three years. In 1802, the boy's father sold the nugget to a jeweler, still not realizing what it was. Later, he learned the value of the nugget, which started the Carolina Gold Rush, the first in the United States.

1317) If Walmart was a country, its revenues would rank it as the 25th largest economy in the world.

1318) Wild chimpanzees in Guinea drink fermented palm sap that contains up to 6.9% alcohol. Some of the chimpanzees consume significant quantities and exhibit signs of inebriation.

1319) In the Humpty Dumpty nursery rhyme, there is no indication that he is an egg. Early illustrations portrayed him as a young boy.

1320) The practice of quarantine began during the 14th century when ships arriving in Venice from plague-infected ports were required to sit at anchor for 40 days before landing. The word quarantine derives from the Italian words "quaranta giorni," which means 40 days.

1321) NASA accidentally erased and reused the original 1969 *Apollo 11* moon landing tapes. The tapes were reused as part of a money-saving effort.

1322) In the 1st century, the Romans had polar bears fight seals in amphitheaters they flooded with water.

1323) You can't really cry in space because there isn't gravity for tears to flow downward. The liquid builds up in a ball in the eye until it is large enough to break free of the eye and float around.

1324) A jellyfish's mouth also serves as its anus.

1325) Even though the human sense of smell is not near as sophisticated as some animals, recent research estimates that the human nose can detect at least 1 trillion different scents.

1326) Worldwide, there are about 107 human deaths per minute, about 1.78 deaths per second.

1327) Due to anti-German sentiment during WWI, the British royal family changed their name to Windsor from Saxe-Coburg and Gotha in 1917, so the family is named after the castle and not the other way around.

1328) In space, blood flow doesn't work the same without gravity. Blood can flow up towards the head instead of pulling down toward the feet. Astronaut's faces typically look puffy from extra blood flow for the first few days until their bodies adapt.

1329) Writing punctuation as we largely know it today did not exist until the 15th century.

1330) Ninety percent of all English written material is made up of just 1,000 words.

1331) The average human worldwide weighs about 137 pounds.

1332) Rome, Italy, is located at about the same latitude as the southernmost point of Canada; by area, it is farther north than 62% of the United States.

1333) The Amazon rainforest is home to 10% of the known species in the world.

1334) The Pacific Ocean side entrance to the Panama Canal is further east than the Atlantic Ocean side entrance.

1335) Jane Addams was the first American woman to win a Nobel Prize; she shared the 1931 Nobel Peace Prize.

1336) An ostrich's eye is bigger than its brain.

1337) In 1898, Morgan Robertson wrote a short novel called *Futility*. It had a large unsinkable ship, called the *Titan,* that carried an insufficient number of lifeboats, and on an April voyage, it hits an iceberg and sinks in the North Atlantic, resulting in the loss of almost everyone on board. Fourteen years later in April 1912, the large unsinkable *Titanic* with an insufficient number of lifeboats hit an iceberg and sank in the North Atlantic, losing most of the people on board.

1338) In 1975, Kodak created the first digital still camera; it weighed 8 pounds and took 0.01-megapixel black-and-white photos that took 23 seconds to render onto a cassette tape that displayed the image on a television set.

1339) Stephen Girard was one of the wealthiest men in American history, and he saved the United States from financial collapse during the War of 1812 by placing most of his assets at the disposal of the government and underwriting about 95% of the war loans.

1340) Bookkeeper and bookkeeping are the only two English words with three consecutive double letters.

1341) It would take about 150 ruby-throated hummingbirds to weigh one pound.

1342) Baby elephants suck their trunk for comfort just like human babies suck their thumb.

1343) The Titanoboa is the largest snake ever known to have existed; it lived about 60 million years ago and was up to 42 feet long and weighed up to 2,500 pounds.

1344) In 1980, the world's first 1-gigabyte disk drive took up the space of a refrigerator, weighed 1,000 pounds, and cost $81,000.

1345) Located in Fez, Morocco, the al-Qarawiyyin library is the world's oldest working library, operating since 859 AD.

1346) Flamingos are naturally white; their brine shrimp and algae diet make them pink.

1347) Cornicione is the name for the outer part of a pizza crust.

1348) In the 1600s, some doctors recommended their patients fart into jars and store it to later inhale to ward off the bubonic plague. The idea was that the plague was caused by deadly vapors, so it could be warded off by foul vapors.

1349) A mononymous person is known and addressed by one name.

1350) Flamingos bend their legs at the ankle and not the knee. Their knee is located much higher up, hidden under their feathers. The whole area from the ankle to the toes is a giant foot. The joint that looks like an ankle, near the bottom of their leg, is the beginning of their toes, so about half of what appears to be the flamingo's legs are really its feet.

1351) Ketchup originated in China many centuries ago; the original sauce was derived from fermented fish. The British picked it up and altered it to be more like a Worcestershire sauce. Tomatoes weren't used in ketchup until the early 19th century in the United States.

1352) It takes about 1,000 years for any cubic meter of ocean water to circulate around the world.

1353) Early Americans used corn cobs for toilet paper. Dried corncobs were plentiful, efficient, and are softer and more flexible than you think.

1354) Written out in English (one, two, three, etc.), eight is the first number alphabetically, no matter how high you go.

1355) Birds are essentially immune to the heat of chili peppers; they don't have the right type or number of taste receptors to be affected.

1356) Snapping shrimp can snap their specialized claw shut producing a cavitation bubble that releases a sound as loud as 218 decibels, louder than a rocket launch. When the bubble collapses, it can reach temperatures of 4,700 degrees Celsius, almost as hot as the surface of the sun.

1357) Albert Einstein described it as "spooky action at a distance" and didn't believe nature would be so unreasonable, but quantum entanglement that occurs when two particles are inextricably linked together, no matter their physical separation, has been proven repeatedly in experiments. Although entangled particles are not physically connected, they are still able to share information instantaneously, breaking the rule that no information can be transmitted faster than the speed of light. In tests, entangled particles 750 miles apart have shown that any change in one is instantly reflected in the other; this would be true even if they were separated by light-years.

1358) Lucy, a star in the constellation Centaurus 50 light-years away, is about 90% crystallized carbon, making it a 10-sextillion-carat diamond.

1359) If you average out the colors of all the stars we can see, you get beige, so the average color of the observable universe is beige.

1360) There are an estimated one million spiders per acre of land; in the tropics, there are closer to three million per acre.

1361) You can fire a gun in the oxygen-free environment of space. Fires can't burn without oxygen, but modern ammunition contains its own oxidizer to trigger the explosion of gunpowder and fire the bullet; no atmospheric oxygen is required.

1362) While only 3.1% of the world's children live in the United States, they own 40% of the toys consumed globally.

1363) In 1776, Margaret Corbin became the first woman recognized as a soldier in the American Revolutionary War; she was also the first woman to receive a U.S. military pension.

1364) There is a southern version of the aurora borealis (northern lights) called the aurora australis; it can be seen from Antarctica, New Zealand, Argentina, and Australia.

1365) A nurdle is the wave-like gob of toothpaste you put on your toothbrush.

1366) Seahorses are very bad swimmers. They propel themselves using a dorsal fin that beats 30-70 times per second. The tiny fin and awkward body shape make it difficult to get around, and they can easily die of exhaustion navigating in stormy water.

1367) Harry S. Truman was the last U.S. president without a college degree.

1368) The coldest temperature ever recorded on the earth was minus 128.56 degrees Fahrenheit on July 21, 1983, at Antarctica's Vostok station.

1369) Insects don't flap their wings as birds do. An insect's wings are attached to its exoskeleton; they contract their muscles and force their whole body to vibrate, which causes the wings to vibrate.

1370) If you have bloodshot eyes after swimming in a pool, it isn't chlorine causing the reaction; it is urine mixing with the pool's chemicals. The nitrogen in urine combines with the chlorine and forms chloramine that causes eye irritation.

1371) To minimize the risk of drowning, dolphins are usually born tail first.

1372) Rats are not likely to blame for transmitting the Black Death bubonic plague that wiped out one-third of Europe's population in the 14th century. Experiments assessing the transmission routes prove that the parasites that carried the disease were much more likely to have come from human fleas and lice.

1373) The tufts of hair in a cat's ear are called ear furnishings; they help keep out dirt, direct sounds, and insulate the ears.

1374) When feeding, a hummingbird can lick 10-15 times per second.

1375) The color orange is named after the fruit and not the other way around.

1376) Opossums are a great help in preventing the spread of Lyme disease. They are fastidiously clean and spend hours cleaning themselves; as they clean their fur, they pick off and swallow ticks, which kills them. Studies have shown a single opossum can destroy 5,000 ticks in a season.

1377) Less than 10% of legally blind Americans can read Braille.

1378) As a defense mechanism when threatened, sea cucumbers can eviscerate themselves and shoot out their internal organs. Sea cucumbers are echinoderms, which also include marine animals like starfish and sea urchins; depending on the species, they can shoot the organs out their head or butt, but they can regrow the organs. Through a process called dedifferentiation, certain cells in their bodies lose their specialized functions and move around the sea cucumber's body and become whatever type of cell is needed to regrow the lost organs.

1379) The division sign (short horizontal line with a dot above and below) in math is called an obelus.

1380) The largest contiguous land empire in history was Genghis Khan's Mongol Empire that spanned 9.27 million square miles in one mass at its peak in 1270. At its peak in 1920, the British Empire was larger but scattered around the world.

1381) Most Japanese schools don't employ janitors or custodians; they believe that requiring students to clean the school teaches respect, responsibility, and promotes equality.

1382) In Boston, Massachusetts, in January 1919, a 50-foot-tall holding tank burst open sending a 15-foot-tall wave of molasses through the streets. It crushed houses and killed 21 people and injured 150.

1383) Statistically, the deadliest job in America is U.S. president; four presidents have been assassinated in office, an 8.9% fatality rate.

1384) Snails slide around on a single foot; the one long muscle acts like a human extremity and helps them grip and push themselves along the ground.

1385) There are about 3 trillion total trees in the world.

1386) Human babies are born without kneecaps; the cartilage in their knee ossifies into kneecaps at three to five years old.

1387) Quetzalcoatlus, from the Late Cretaceous period, is the largest known flying animal to have ever lived. It had a wingspan up to 36 feet and may have weighed as much as 500 pounds.

1388) To ensure global supply in the case of an emergency, Canada has a strategic maple syrup reserve. The reserve contains about 2.4 million gallons of syrup; Quebec province produces about 75% of the global supply of maple syrup.

1389) The tallest married couple ever were Canadian Anna Haining Swan, who was 7'11", and American Martin Van Buren Bates, who was 7'9". The couple was married in 1871, and Swan later gave birth to a 22-pound baby.

1390) Snail slime is mucus that lubricates the surface and helps them move faster with less friction; they often travel in the mucus trails of other snails to move faster.

1391) Movie trailers originally played after the movie; that is why they were called trailers.

1392) The term jaywalker originated because jay was a term for an idiot or simpleton and was often applied to rural people; therefore, jaywalking was being stupid, ignoring signs, and crossing the street in an unsafe place.

1393) The average American professional football game lasts 3 hours and 12 minutes but only has about 11 minutes when the ball is in play.

1394) If you measure from base to summit, Hawaii's Mauna Kea is the tallest mountain in the world. Measured from the seafloor where it starts, Mauna Kea is about 33,500 feet tall, almost 4,500 feet taller than Mount Everest, but it only reaches 13,796 feet above sea level.

1395) Crocodiles and alligators can climb trees. Researchers have found adults as high as 6 feet off the ground, and juveniles have been spotted as high as 30 feet.

1396) Ancient Roman public toilets had a long marble bench with holes on top where you sat and holes in the front for the sponge on a stick used to clean yourself after. There were no doors or dividing walls; you sat right next to someone else. Once you had done your business, you would rinse the sponge in the channel of running water at your feet, push the sponge on a stick through the hole in the front and wipe yourself, and then rinse off the sponge and leave it in a basin for the next person.

1397) Eleven states have land farther south than the most northern part of Mexico: Alabama, Arizona, California, Florida, Georgia, Hawaii, Louisiana, Mississippi, New Mexico, South Carolina, and Texas.

1398) If sound waves could travel through space as they do through air, you would hear the sun burning at a volume of about 100 decibels, about the same volume as a chainsaw or jackhammer. Sound intensity decreases with distance, so the 93 million miles to the sun has a large impact on the volume.

1399) The Brothers Grimm version of *Cinderella* is a much darker story; the stepsisters cut off their toe and a part of their heel to fit into the shoe, and they try to go to Cinderella's wedding and get their eyes plucked out by birds.

1400) Corn, rice, and wheat account for about 51% of the world's calorie intake.

1401) The metal part of a pencil that holds the eraser in place is called the ferrule.

1402) The geographic center of the contiguous United States is two miles northwest of the town of Lebanon, Kansas, on a pig farm.

1403) You will never actually see yourself; you only see representations of yourself or a flipped image in a mirror.

1404) Sharks have a very well-developed sense of hearing. Their ears are small holes on the sides of their head that lead directly to the inner ear. They are particularly good at hearing low-frequency noises, such as an injured fish would make, and at finding out where a noise is coming from.

1405) Dr. James Naismith, who invented the game of basketball in 1891, is the only Kansas Jayhawk men's basketball coach in history with a losing record. He founded the University of Kansas basketball program, where he became the Kansas coach and athletic director.

1406) After dropping out 34 years earlier, Steven Spielberg got his Bachelor of Arts degree from Cal State Long Beach; they gave him course credit for paleontology for the work he did on *Jurassic Park*.

1407) If you started with $0.01 and had a 100% daily return on your money, you would be a millionaire in 27 days.

1408) Each minute, an adult male human loses about 96 million cells that are replaced by cells dividing.

1409) The pineapple is a berry; it produces hundreds of flowers that produce fruits and coalesce into a single larger fruit.

1410) The highest and lowest points in the contiguous United States are in the same county. Mount Whitney, at 14,494 feet, and the Badwater Basin in Death Valley, at 282 feet below sea level, are separated by 85 miles in Inyo County California.

1411) A group of butterflies is called a kaleidoscope.

1412) The first food ever microwaved on purpose was popcorn. In 1945, Raytheon patented the first microwave oven; engineer Percy Spencer had first discovered the heating powers of microwaves when he accidentally melted a candy bar in his pocket. He tested it out officially on popcorn, which was a success, and on an egg, which exploded.

1413) All humans are about 99.9% genetically the same.

1414) A vast reservoir of water, three times the volume of all the oceans, is located about 400 miles beneath the earth's crust. The water is locked up in a mineral called ringwoodite.

1415) An average alligator can go through 2,000 to 3,000 teeth in a lifetime. An alligator has roughly 80 teeth, and as the teeth wear down, they are replaced.

1416) Central America's Lake Nicaragua is one of the very few freshwater lakes in the world with sharks. Bull sharks can survive in both fresh and saltwater and make their way back and forth from the

Caribbean Sea to Lake Nicaragua via a 120-mile route through the San Juan river. Researchers have tagged sharks and verified that they move back and forth between the lake and the sea.

1417) The heat index is a measure of the discomfort the average person experiences because of the combined effects of air temperature and humidity. The world's highest recorded heat index was 178 at Dhahran, Saudi Arabia, on July 8, 2003, with a temperature of 108 and a dew point of 95.

1418) Bananas, along with other potassium-rich foods like spinach, apricots, salmon, avocados, and mushrooms, are radioactive. K-40 radioactive atoms make up a very small fraction of potassium atoms; they spontaneously decay, releasing beta radiation and gamma rays which are both capable of tissue damage. However, K-40 is not very radioactive, with a half-life of 1.3 billion years, so you would have to eat about 10 million bananas to die of radiation poisoning.

1419) Avocados don't ripen on the tree. They only ripen once they are off the tree, so the trees can be used as storage and will keep avocados fresh for up to seven months.

1420) The boa constrictor is the only living animal that has the same common and scientific name.

1421) The average pencil has enough graphite to draw a line 35 miles long or write about 45,000 words.

1422) The Appalachian Mountains used to be as tall as the Rockies and are still shrinking; meanwhile, the Himalayas used to be the size of the Rockies and are still growing.

1423) There are about 2.5 human births for every death in the world.

1424) After going deaf, Beethoven discovered he could bite on a metal pole connected to the piano he was playing and hear almost perfectly. This process is known as bone conduction; vibrations are transferred into the bones, and the ears pick up the signal with no sound distortion, bypassing the eardrums. We all hear sounds through both our bones and our eardrums; most sounds are air conducted, where the eardrum converts sound waves to vibrations and transmits them to the inner ear. In some cases, vibrations are heard directly by the inner ear, bypassing your eardrums; this is one of the ways you hear your own voice.

1425) The Fitzroy River turtle, a species that can only be found in the Fitzroy River in Australia, can breathe through its anus. They are constantly pumping water in and out of their anus, collecting as much as 70% of the oxygen they need to survive. Consequently, they can stay underwater for up to three weeks at a time. They are not the only turtle species that can breathe through its anus, but they can use the function to a greater extent.

1426) Less than 1% of dreams contain smell, taste, or pain elements. Most dreams contain visual and movement features, and half of all dreams contain auditory elements.

1427) A shark can have over 30,000 teeth in its lifetime. A shark's teeth are arranged in rows, with each successive row smaller than the last. On average, they have 15 rows of teeth, with some species having up to 50 rows. The row nearest the front is the largest and most used. If a shark loses a tooth, the tooth in the row behind it moves up to take its place. A shark's teeth are not embedded in its jaw; they are attached to the skin covering the jaw. New teeth are continually being grown in a groove in the shark's mouth, and the skin moves the teeth forward into new positions. If they couldn't quickly replace their teeth, they wouldn't have been able to develop such a strong bite, which causes them to lose so many teeth.

1428) At normal atmospheric pressure, helium is the only element in the universe that can't freeze; it can't get cold enough.

1429) In 1890, Wyoming became the first state to give women the right to vote; as a territory, it had given women the right to vote in 1869.

1430) Margaret Abbott was the first American woman to win an Olympic gold medal; at the 1900 Paris Olympics, she won the women's golf tournament.

1431) The largest waterfall in the world is underwater. The Denmark Strait cataract is located between Greenland and Iceland and is 100 miles long and drops 11,500 feet from the Greenland Sea into the Irminger Sea. It is three times taller than Angel Falls in Venezuela and has 2,000 times more water than Niagara Falls. The cataract is formed by the difference in temperature between the cold Arctic waters of the Greenland Sea and the slightly warmer Irminger Sea. When the waters meet, the colder Greenland Sea water falls to the bottom.

1432) By looking at a variety of animal species, a study found that as an animal's brain gets larger, its yawn gets longer.

1433) To get the stunning detail in his bird paintings, John James Audubon would often kill the subject and pose it, so he could create realistic paintings without the subject flying away.

1434) Turritopsis dohrnii, also known as the immortal jellyfish, is essentially biologically immortal. Once the adult jellyfish have reproduced, they transform themselves back into their juvenile state. Their tentacles retract; their bodies shrink, and they sink to the ocean floor and start their life cycle all over again. They can do it repeatedly, making them essentially immortal unless they are consumed by another fish or struck by a disease.

1435) You can always see your nose, but you don't see it unless you think about it. The process is called unconscious selective attention and allows the brain to block out distractions.

1436) The color of an egg has nothing to do with nutrition, quality, or flavor. In general, white-feathered chickens with white earlobes lay white eggs, and reddish-brown-feathered chickens with red earlobes lay brown eggs.

1437) Cats don't have very good close vision, so when they are near water, they may not be able to see the water or the water level. That is why they will frequently paw the water to feel the level or move the dish to cause a disturbance in the water, so they can see it.

1438) A rat can tread water for three days and survive being flushed down the toilet.

1439) In 2012, scientists discovered a new species of ant that appears to live exclusively in New York City. The ant was discovered where Broadway meets 63rd street and 76th street and is called the ManhattAnt. They believe it has evolved to adapt to its warmer, drier, concrete-covered environment.

1440) A contronym is a word with two opposite meanings; for example, clip can mean to fasten or detach.

1441) If you wrapped a rope around the earth's equator tightly hugging the ground, you would only need to add about 6.3 feet of rope for it to hover one foot above the ground around the earth.

1442) Even though it is the same size, the moon appears to be larger when it is nearer the horizon than when it is higher in the sky. This is known as the Moon Illusion and has been known since ancient times. There is no consensus on what causes the illusion, but the most important factor is likely that terrain and other objects are in view along with the moon and impact the perception of distance and size when it is nearer the horizon.

1443) As a gas, oxygen is odorless and colorless; in its liquid and solid forms, it looks pale blue.

1444) Buddha, Confucius, and Socrates all lived about the same time. Buddha is believed to have died in 483 BC; Confucius died in 479 BC, and Socrates was born in 469 BC.

1445) The Great Barrier Reef is the largest living structure on the earth. Situated off the northeastern coast of Australia, it stretches for 1,429 miles and covers an area of approximately 133,000 square miles.

1446) The longest English word in any major dictionary is the 45-letter pneumonoultramicroscopicsilicovolcanoconiosis, a lung disease caused by inhalation of silicate or quartz dust.

1447) The first automatically sliced commercial bread was produced in 1928 in Missouri.

1448) The sword-billed hummingbird is the only bird with a bill longer than its body.

1449) Blood can be used as an egg substitute in cooking. Blood and eggs have a similar protein composition, particularly with albumin that gives both their coagulant properties. In tests, 65 grams of blood was substituted for one egg.

1450) In a show of dominance, male Indian rhinos can spray urine over 16 feet; this is typically done in the presence of other males or breeding-age females.

1451) It takes about 90 minutes to hard boil an ostrich egg.

1452) When playing with female puppies, male puppies will often let the female win, even if they have a physical advantage.

1453) Circus Maximus, the ancient Roman venue for chariot racing, could seat 250,000 spectators. The track was 540 meters long by 80 meters wide and had 12 chariot starting gates. It was constructed in the 6th century BC, and the last chariot races were held there in the 6th century AD.

1454) In 1999, NASA estimated that antimatter cost $28 quadrillion per pound to produce.

1455) Bumblebees have been found at altitudes as high as 18,000 feet, and tests have shown that they can fly at over 29,000 feet.

1456) The zombie ant fungi can hijack an ant's central nervous and force the ant to do what it wants. When an ant contacts the fungal spores, the fungus infects the ant and quickly spreads throughout its body. Fungal cells in the ant's head release chemicals that hijack the ant's central nervous system. The fungus forces the ant to climb up vegetation and clamp down onto a leaf or twig before killing it. After the ant is dead, the fungus grows a spore releasing stalk out of the back of the ant's head that infects more ants on the ground below.

1457) Humans aren't either left-brained or right-brained as once thought; most behaviors and abilities require the right and left sides of the brain to work together. You have characteristics and abilities that define who you are, but they have nothing to do with which side of the brain you use more.

1458) Cheetahs can't roar; they can purr, meow, hiss, bark, and growl.

1459) Pareidolia is the term for seeing patterns in random data. Some common examples are seeing a likeness in the clouds or an image on the surface of the moon.

1460) Robins can eat up to 14 feet of earthworms in a day.

1461) In 1898, Nikola Tesla created the first remote control that could control mechanical devices at a distance with radio waves. The first electronic television wasn't invented until 1927, and the first wireless television remote wasn't created until 1956.

1462) UY Scuti, a bright red supergiant star in the Scutum constellation about 9,500 light-years away, is believed to be the largest star in the Milky Way Galaxy. Its volume is about 27.3 quadrillion times larger than the earth, and its radius is about 1,700 times larger than the sun.

1463) Like other mammals and all air-breathing vertebrates studied to date, adult humans have a diving reflex. The diving reflex is triggered when the nostrils become chilled and wet while holding your breath. The body reacts with slowed heart rate, redirection of blood to the vital organs to conserve oxygen, and a release of red blood cells stored in the spleen, enabling the body to survive submersion for a longer time.

1464) The 10,000-ton meteor that struck Russia in 2013 had an estimated impact energy of 500 kilotons and affected an area of 77,000 square miles. The atomic bomb dropped on Hiroshima was about 33 times smaller.

1465) Even rarer than a double rainbow, a twinned rainbow has two separate and concentric rainbow arcs splitting from a single base. Unlike a double rainbow, both rainbows have their colors in the same order. Twinned rainbows occur with a combination of different size raindrops; due to air resistance, raindrops flatten as they fall, with larger drops flattening more. If there are two rain showers with different size drops, they can combine to form a twinned rainbow.

1466) Cicadas flex their muscles to buckle a series of ribs one after another to produce their loud sound. Every time a rib buckles, it produces a click; many clicks produce the buzzing sound. The series of ribs are called a tymbal.

1467) Lobsters don't have blood like vertebrate animals. The liquid found in their body that acts as blood is called hemolymph; it is colorless and turns blue when exposed to air due to oxygen reacting with the copper in the fluid.

1468) Submarines made their first wartime appearance during the American Revolutionary War. On Sept. 6, 1776, *Turtle*, a submersible built by American David Bushnell, was used in an attempted attack on the British ship *Eagle*. It was a one-man wooden craft that relied on a human-powered hand crank and foot treadle for propulsion. A pedal-operated water tank allowed it to submerge and surface, and lead ballast kept it upright in the water.

1469) For humans, the rarest hair and eye color combination in the world is red hair and blue eyes that account for only about 0.17% of the population. The combination is so rare because both red hair and blue eyes are recessive traits, where both parents must carry the gene for the child to have it.

1470) Astronomers have discovered the largest reservoir of water ever detected in the universe; it has the equivalent of 140 trillion times all the water in the earth's oceans and surrounds a huge black hole, more than 12 billion light-years away.

1471) In 1881, the United States had three presidents. Rutherford B. Hayes started the year as president and was succeeded by James A. Garfield in March after his election. Chester A. Arthur, Garfield's vice president, became president in September after Garfield's assassination.

1472) Even though it is the third most common element in the earth's crust, aluminum was more valuable than gold in the 1800s because it was so rare. Aluminum is seldom found in its pure form, and it is difficult to extract from ores, so before more efficient processes were developed to extract it, aluminum was quite rare. In the 1850s, aluminum was priced at $1,200 per kilogram, and gold was priced at $664 per kilogram.

1473) Sloths are good swimmers; using a version of a dog paddle, they can swim up to three times as fast as they move on land.

1474) On average, humans swallow twice a minute, even while sleeping.

1475) The Amazon River has the largest discharge volume of any river in the world. At an average of about 55 million gallons per second, its discharge is larger than the next seven largest rivers in the world combined and accounts for 20% of the total global river discharge to the oceans.

1476) Victoria Island, in the Canadian territory of Nunavut, has the largest island-in-a-lake-on-an-island-in-a-lake-on-an-island in the world. Victoria Island is the eighth largest island in the world; the final, smallest island is four acres.

1477) Without the impact of gravity, astronauts can become up to two inches taller in space.

1478) Saying "God bless you" when someone sneezes can be traced to a 6th-century order by Pope Gregory I. A pandemic was spreading across the eastern Roman Empire, and the first symptom was severe, chronic sneezing, quickly followed by death. Pope Gregory urged people to pray for the sick and ordered that responses to sneezes should be "God bless you."

1479) The average major league baseball lasts for six pitches.

1480) A sneeze sounds different in different parts of the world. Americans typically say "achoo!"; for Germans, it is "hatschi!"; for Spanish, it is "achis!"; for Japanese, it is "hakashun!"; for Russians, it is "apchkhi!"; for French, it is "atchoum!"

1481) Overmorrow is the day after tomorrow.

1482) Forty-three buildings in New York City are so big that they have their own ZIP Code.

1483) From a standing position, pigs are physically incapable of looking up towards the sky.

1484) Whispering is harder on your vocal cords than normal speech.

1485) Floccinaucinihilipilification is one of the longer words in the English language and means the action of estimating something as worthless.

1486) The Tower of Pisa took 177 years to build, but it started leaning, due to soil subsidence, just 10 years after its completion in 1372. The lean was 5.5 degrees before a 2010 restoration that reduced it to 4 degrees.

1487) Prairie dogs greet each other by kissing; the kiss involves touching their teeth together to determine whether the prairie dog they are greeting is a member of their social group.

1488) It took over 200,000 years for the world's human population to reach one billion, but it only took 200 more years to reach 7 billion.

1489) Lightning strikes the earth's surface about 100 times per second.

1490) Standing up to 6 feet tall and weighing up to 130 pounds, cassowaries are the second largest bird in the world. With a four-inch, dagger-like claw on each foot that can slice open a predator with a single kick, they are also one of the most dangerous birds and have killed humans. They can run up to 31 mph and are native to the tropical forests of Papua New Guinea, Indonesia, and northeastern Australia.

1491) Without an air circulation system, a flame in zero gravity, even in a pure oxygen environment, will extinguish itself. A typical flame produces light, heat, carbon dioxide, and water vapor; the heat causes the combustion products to expand, lowering their density, and they rise, allowing fresh, oxygen-containing air to get to the flame. In zero gravity, nether buoyancy nor convection occurs; therefore, the combustion products accumulate around the flame, preventing oxygen from reaching it, and the flame goes out.

1492) To get a narcotic hit and ward off insects, lemurs in Madagascar capture large red millipedes. When millipedes are picked up, they secrete a toxic combination of chemicals, including cyanide, as a defense mechanism. Lemurs pick up a millipede, bite it gently, and throw it back on the ground; they rub the millipede secretion all over their fur, which functions as a natural pesticide and wards off malaria-carrying mosquitos. The secretion also acts as a narcotic that causes the lemurs to salivate profusely and enter a state of intoxication.

1493) The competition between dogs and cats goes back millions of years; about 20 million years ago in North America, it appears that early cats led to the extinction of most of the ancient dogs.

1494) Astronauts in space are exposed to radiation that is the equivalent of up to 6,000 chest x-rays.

1495) The largest single living organism in the world is a honey mushroom in Malheur National Forest in Oregon. It covers more than three square miles, weighs at least 7,500 tons, and is at least 2,000 years old. For most of the year, the honey mushroom is a thin white layer of fungus that spreads up under a tree's bark and rots its roots, eventually killing the tree over possibly decades. DNA testing has confirmed it is the same organism that has spread from a single location thousands of years ago.

1496) Thomas Andrews, one of the designers of the *Titanic*, was on board when it went down, and his body was never recovered. His suggestions that the ship should have 46 lifeboats instead of 20, a double hull, and a larger number of watertight bulkheads were overruled.

1497) Genghis Khan once ordered his army to eat every tenth man. In 1214, Khan laid siege to the city of Chengdu, the capital of the Chinese Jin empire. The siege went on for a long time, and the Mongols' supplies were short; they were also ravaged by the plague. Khan ordered that every tenth man be sacrificed to feed the others. Khan later personally abandoned the siege, leaving it to one of his generals, and Chengdu eventually fell in 1215.

1498) It wasn't always pink for girls and blue for boys; at one time, it was even reversed. Pink for girls and blue for boys didn't take hold until the middle of the 20th century. Earlier, it was common practice for children to wear gender-neutral, mostly white, clothing. When department stores started marketing gender-specific colors, some early advertising suggested pink for boys since it was considered a stronger color and blue for girls since it was more delicate and daintier.

1499) For more than 150 million years, tiny mammals lived alongside dinosaurs. They were small nocturnal animals, and they remained relatively small until the demise of the dinosaurs 65 million years ago left more niches for them to fill.

1500) Martin Van Buren is the only U.S. president that did not speak English as their first language. Van Buren, who was president from 1837-1841, grew up in the Dutch community of Kinderhook, New York, and spoke Dutch as a child; he learned English as a second language while attending school.

Made in the USA
Columbia, SC
30 November 2020